# enVision® Mathematics
## Common Core

**Volume 1** Topics 1-8

## Authors

**Randall I. Charles**
Professor Emeritus
Department of Mathematics
San Jose State University
San Jose, California

**Jennifer Bay-Williams**
Professor of Mathematics Education
College of Education and Human
Development
University of Louisville
Louisville, Kentucky

**Robert Q. Berry, III**
Professor of Mathematics Education
Department of Curriculum,
Instruction and Special Education
University of Virginia
Charlottesville, Virginia

**Janet H. Caldwell**
Professor Emerita
Department of Mathematics
Rowan University
Glassboro, New Jersey

**Zachary Champagne**
Assistant in Research
Florida Center for Research in Science,
Technology, Engineering, and
Mathematics (FCR-STEM)
Jacksonville, Florida

**Juanita Copley**
Professor Emerita, College of Education
University of Houston
Houston, Texas

**Warren Crown**
Professor Emeritus of Mathematics
Education
Graduate School of Education
Rutgers University
New Brunswick, New Jersey

**Francis (Skip) Fennell**
Professor Emeritus of
Education and Graduate and
Professional Studies
McDaniel College
Westminster, Maryland

**Karen Karp**
Professor of
Mathematics Education
School of Education
Johns Hopkins University
Baltimore, Maryland

**Stuart J. Murphy**
Visual Learning Specialist
Boston, Massachusetts

**Jane F. Schielack**
Professor Emerita
Department of Mathematics
Texas A&M University
College Station, Texas

**Jennifer M. Suh**
Associate Professor for
Mathematics Education
George Mason University
Fairfax, Virginia

**Jonathan A. Wray**
Mathematics Supervisor
Howard County Public Schools
Ellicott City, Maryland

**SAVVAS**
LEARNING COMPANY

## Mathematicians

**Roger Howe**
Professor of Mathematics
Yale University
New Haven, Connecticut

**Gary Lippman**
Professor of Mathematics and
Computer Science
California State University, East Bay
Hayward, California

## ELL Consultants

**Janice R. Corona**
Independent Education Consultant
Dallas, Texas

**Jim Cummins**
Professor
The University of Toronto
Toronto, Canada

## Reviewers

**Katina Arnold**
Teacher
Liberty Public School District
Kansas City, Missouri

**Christy Bennett**
Elementary Math and Science
Specialist
DeSoto County Schools
Hernando, Mississippi

**Shauna Bostick**
Elementary Math Specialist
Lee County School District
Tupelo, Mississippi

**Samantha Brant**
Teacher
Platte County School District
Platte City, Missouri

**Jamie Clark**
Elementary Math Coach
Allegany County Public Schools
Cumberland, Maryland

**Shauna Gardner**
Math and Science Instructional Coach
DeSoto County Schools
Hernando, Mississippi

**Kathy Graham**
Educational Consultant
Twin Falls, Idaho

**Andrea Hamilton**
K-5 Math Specialist
Lake Forest School District
Felton, Delaware

**Susan Hankins**
Instructional Coach
Tupelo Public School District
Tupelo, Mississippi

**Barb Jamison**
Teacher
Excelsior Springs School District
Excelsior Springs, Missouri

**Pam Jones**
Elementary Math Coach
Lake Region School District
Bridgton, Maine

**Sherri Kane**
Secondary Mathematics
Curriculum Specialist
Lee's Summit R7 School District
Lee's Summit, Missouri

**Jessica Leonard**
ESOL Teacher
Volusia County Schools
DeLand, Florida

**Jill K. Milton**
Elementary Math Coordinator
Norwood Public Schools
Norwood, Massachusetts

**Jamie Pickett**
Teacher
Platte County School District
Kansas City, Missouri

**Mandy Schall**
Math Coach
Allegany County Public Schools
Cumberland, Maryland

**Marjorie Stevens**
Math Consultant
Utica Community Schools
Shelby Township, Michigan

**Shyree Stevenson**
ELL Teacher
Penns Grove-Carneys Point
Regional School District
Penns Grove, New Jersey

**Kayla Stone**
Teacher
Excelsior Springs School District
Excelsior Springs, Missouri

**Sara Sultan**
PD Academic Trainer, Math
Tucson Unified School District
Tucson, Arizona

**Angela Waltrup**
Elementary Math Content Specialist
Washington County Public Schools
Hagerstown, Maryland

ISBN-13: 978-0-13-495469-1
ISBN-10: 0-13-495469-6

You'll be using these digital resources throughout the year!

# Digital Resources

Go to SavvasRealize.com

 **Interactive Student Edition**
Access online or offline.

 **Interactive Additional Practice Workbook**
Access online or offline.

 **Math Tools**
Explore math with digital tools.

**Assessment**
Show what you've learned.

 **Visual Learning**
Interact with visual learning animations.

 **Videos**
Watch Math Practices Animations, Another Look Videos, and clips to support 3-Act Math.

**Games**
Play math games to help you learn.

 **Activity**
Solve a problem and share your thinking.

 **Practice Buddy**
Do interactice practice online.

 **Glossary**
Read and listen in English and Spanish.

**SAVVAS realize**™ Everything you need for math anytime, anywhere

# Contents

**Digital Resources at SavvasRealize.com**

## TOPICS

And remember your Interactive Student Edition is available at SavvasRealize.com!

SavvasRealize.com

This shows how you can use ten-frames to make a 10.

# TOPIC 1
## Fluently Add and Subtract Within 20

**Contents**

This shows how you can use connecting cubes to show that a number is even or odd.

8 is even.
4 + 4 = 8

9 is odd.
5 + 4 = 9

# TOPIC 2
## Work with Equal Groups

This shows how you can add two-digit numbers using a hundred chart.

$$54 + 18 = 72$$

| 51 | 52 | 53 | 54 | 55 | 56 | 57 | 58 | 59 | 60 |
|----|----|----|----|----|----|----|----|----|----|
| 61 | 62 | 63 | 64 | 65 | 66 | 67 | 68 | 69 | 70 |
| 71 | 72 | 73 | 74 | 75 | 76 | 77 | 78 | 79 | 80 |

# TOPIC 3
## Add Within 100 Using Strategies

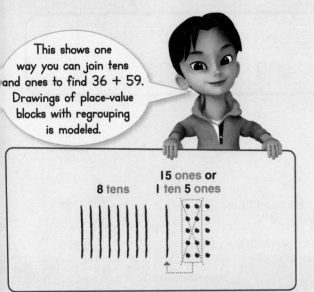

This shows one way you can join tens and ones to find 36 + 59. Drawings of place-value blocks with regrouping is modeled.

8 tens

15 ones or
1 ten 5 ones

# TOPIC 4
## Fluently Add Within 100

SavvasRealize.com

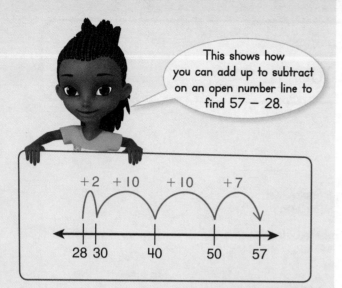

This shows how you can add up to subtract on an open number line to find 57 − 28.

+2  +10    +10    +7

28 30    40    50    57

# TOPIC 5
# Subtract Within 100 Using Strategies

Contents

This shows how you can use place-value blocks to find 34 − 6 using regrouping.

| Tens | Ones |
|------|------|

2 tens    8 ones

# TOPIC 6
## Fluently Subtract Within 100

SavvasRealize.com

**Contents**

This shows how bar diagrams can be used to model and solve a two-step problem.

Mia sees 15 yellow birds and 16 red birds. Some birds fly away and now Mia sees 14 birds. How many birds flew away?

# TOPIC 7
## More Solving Problems Involving Addition and Subtraction

This shows how you can count on to find the total value.

Micah has the coins shown below. How many cents does Micah have?

50¢   75¢   85¢   90¢   91¢

# TOPIC 8
## Work with Time and Money

SavvasRealize.com

# Grade 2 Common Core Standards

Dear Families,

The standards on the following pages describe the math that students will learn this year.

## DOMAIN 2.OA
## OPERATIONS AND ALGEBRAIC THINKING

### MAJOR CLUSTER 2.OA.A
**Represent and solve problems involving addition and subtraction.**

**2.OA.A.1** Use addition and subtraction within 100 to solve one- and two-step word problems involving situations of adding to, taking from, putting together, taking apart, and comparing, with unknowns in all positions, e.g., by using drawings and equations with a symbol for the unknown number to represent the problem.

### MAJOR CLUSTER 2.OA.B
**Add and subtract within 20.**

**2.OA.B.2** Fluently add and subtract within 20 using mental strategies. By end of Grade 2, know from memory all sums of two one-digit numbers.

### SUPPORTING CLUSTER 2.OA.C
**Work with equal groups of objects to gain foundations for multiplication.**

**2.OA.C.3** Determine whether a group of objects (up to 20) has an odd or even number of members, e.g., by pairing objects or counting them by 2s; write an equation to express an even number as a sum of two equal addends.

**2.OA.C.4** Use addition to find the total number of objects arranged in rectangular arrays with up to 5 rows and up to 5 columns; write an equation to express the total as a sum of equal addends.

# Common Core Standards

## DOMAIN 2.NBT
## NUMBER AND OPERATIONS IN BASE TEN

### MAJOR CLUSTER 2.NBT.A
**Understand place value.**

**2.NBT.A.1** Understand that the three digits of a three-digit number represent amounts of hundreds, tens, and ones; e.g., 706 equals 7 hundreds, 0 tens, and 6 ones. Understand the following as special cases:

**2.NBT.A.1a** 100 can be thought of as a bundle of ten tens—called a "hundred."

**2.NBT.A.1b** The numbers 100, 200, 300, 400, 500, 600, 700, 800, 900 refer to one, two, three, four, five, six, seven, eight, or nine hundreds (and 0 tens and 0 ones).

**2.NBT.A.2** Count within 1000; skip-count by 5s, 10s, and 100s.

**2.NBT.A.3** Read and write numbers to 1000 using base-ten numerals, number names, and expanded form.

**2.NBT.A.4** Compare two three-digit numbers based on meanings of the hundreds, tens, and ones digits, using >, =, and < symbols to record the results of comparisons.

### MAJOR CLUSTER 2.NBT.B
**Use place value understanding and properties of operations to add and subtract.**

**2.NBT.B.5** Fluently add and subtract within 100 using strategies based on place value, properties of operations, and/or the relationship between addition and subtraction.

**2.NBT.B.6** Add up to four two-digit numbers using strategies based on place value and properties of operations.

**2.NBT.B.7** Add and subtract within 1000, using concrete models or drawings and strategies based on place value, properties of operations, and/or the relationship between addition and subtraction; relate the strategy to a written method. Understand that in adding or subtracting three-digit numbers, one adds or subtracts hundreds and hundreds, tens and tens, ones and ones; and sometimes it is necessary to compose or decompose tens or hundreds.

**2.NBT.B.8** Mentally add 10 or 100 to a given number 100–900, and mentally subtract 10 or 100 from a given number 100–900.

**2.NBT.B.9** Explain why addition and subtraction strategies work, using place value and the properties of operations.[1]

# Common Core Standards

## DOMAIN 2.MD
## MEASUREMENT AND DATA

### MAJOR CLUSTER 2.MD.A
**Measure and estimate lengths in standard units.**

**2.MD.A.1** Measure the length of an object by selecting and using appropriate tools such as rulers, yardsticks, meter sticks, and measuring tapes.

**2.MD.A.2** Measure the length of an object twice, using length units of different lengths for the two measurements; describe how the two measurements relate to the size of the unit chosen.

**2.MD.A.3** Estimate lengths using units of inches, feet, centimeters, and meters.

**2.MD.A.4** Measure to determine how much longer one object is than another, expressing the length difference in terms of a standard length unit.

### MAJOR CLUSTER 2.MD.B
**Relate addition and subtraction to length.**

**2.MD.B.5** Use addition and subtraction within 100 to solve word problems involving lengths that are given in the same units, e.g., by using drawings (such as drawings of rulers) and equations with a symbol for the unknown number to represent the problem.

**2.MD.B.6** Represent whole numbers as lengths from 0 on a number line diagram with equally spaced points corresponding to the numbers 0, 1, 2, ..., and represent whole-number sums and differences within 100 on a number line diagram.

### SUPPORTING CLUSTER 2.MD.C
**Work with time and money.**

**2.MD.C.7** Tell and write time from analog and digital clocks to the nearest five minutes, using A.M. and P.M.

**2.MD.C.8** Solve word problems involving dollar bills, quarters, dimes, nickels, and pennies, using $ and ¢ symbols appropriately. *Example: If you have 2 dimes and 3 pennies, how many cents do you have?*

### SUPPORTING CLUSTER 2.MD.D
**Represent and interpret data.**

**2.MD.D.9** Generate measurement data by measuring lengths of several objects to the nearest whole unit, or by making repeated measurements of the same object. Show the measurements by making a line plot, where the horizontal scale is marked off in whole-number units.

**2.MD.D.10** Draw a picture graph and a bar graph (with single-unit scale) to represent a data set with up to four categories. Solve simple put-together, take-apart, and compare problems using information presented in a bar graph.

# Common Core Standards

## DOMAIN 2.G
## GEOMETRY

### ADDITIONAL CLUSTER 2.G.A
**Reason with shapes and their attributes.**

**2.G.A.1** Recognize and draw shapes having specified attributes, such as a given number of angles or a given number of equal faces.[2] Identify triangles, quadrilaterals, pentagons, hexagons, and cubes.

**2.MD.A.2** Partition a rectangle into rows and columns of same-size squares and count to find the total number of them.

**2.MD.A.3** Partition circles and rectangles into two, three, or four equal shares, describe the shares using the words *halves*, *thirds*, *half of*, *a third of*, etc., and describe the whole as two halves, three thirds, four fourths. Recognize that equal shares of identical wholes need not have the same shape.

[1]Explanations may be supported by drawings or objects.

[2]Sizes are compared directly or visually, not compared by measuring.

## MATHEMATICAL PRACTICES

**MP.1** Make sense of problems and persevere in solving them.

**MP.2** Reason abstractly and quantitatively.

**MP.3** Construct viable arguments and critique the reasoning of others.

**MP.4** Model with mathematics.

**MP.5** Use appropriate tools strategically.

**MP.6** Attend to precision.

**MP.7** Look for and make use of structure.

**MP.8** Look for and express regularity in repeated reasoning.

# Math Practices and Problem Solving Handbook

The **Math Practices and Problem Solving Handbook** is available at SavvasRealize.com.

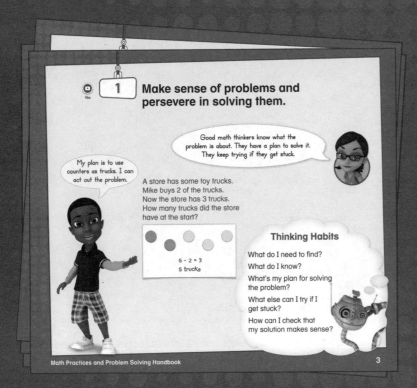

**Math Practices**

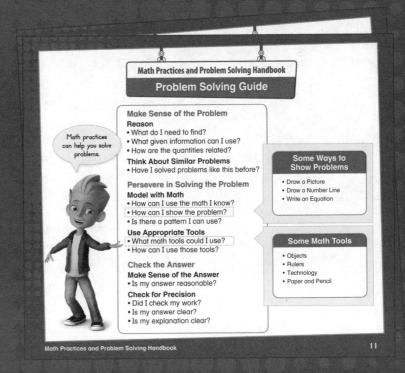

**Problem Solving Guide**
**Problem Solving Recording Sheet**

# Fluently Add and Subtract Within 20

**Essential Question:** What are strategies for finding addition and subtraction facts?

Look at the different types of paper!

Different papers have different properties.

Wow! Let's do this project and learn more.

## enVision STEM Project: Material Math

**Find Out** Collect different types of paper. Talk about the uses of paper. Tell how strong each type of paper is. Tell how the paper feels. Tell if the paper can soak up water.

**Journal: Make a Book** Show what you find out in a book. In your book, also:

- Glue samples of paper and tell what you found.

- Choose a type of paper to make flash cards of addition and subtraction facts.

Name _Umarbek_

# Review What You Know

## A-Z Vocabulary

**1.** Circle the symbol for **equals**.

$-$

$+$

$\boxed{=}$

**2.** Circle the symbol for **minus**.

$\ominus$

$+$

$=$

**3.** Circle the number that is the **whole**.

$4 + 2 = \boxed{6}$

## Subtraction Stories

**4.** There are 7 birds on a fence. 2 fly away. How many birds are left?

_5_ birds

## Addition Stories

**5.** Write an equation to solve the problem.

Kate draws 4 big stars. Then she draws 2 small stars. How many stars does Kate draw in all?

$4 + 2 = 6$

## Make 10

**6.** Write an equation that shows this way to make a 10.

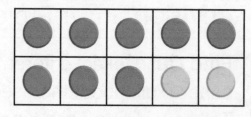

$8 + 2 = 0$

**2** two

Topic 1

Name _____

**PROJECT 1A**

## What has 8 legs and is big and hairy?

**Project:** Make an Insect and Spider Poster

**PROJECT 1B**

## What are some fun water facts?

**Project:** Collect Water Data

**PROJECT 1C**

## Have you seen this different kind of art?

**Project:** Create a Shape Collage

## Math Modeling
### Losing Marbles

Video

Before watching the video, talk to a classmate:

Who has more pets? Who has fewer siblings? What's something you both have the same number of? We can compare just about anything!

## I can ...
model with math to solve a problem that involves adding and subtracting.

© **Mathematical Practices** MP.4
Also MP.3, MP.8
**Content Standards** 2.OA.A.1
Also 2.OA.B.2

**Solve & Share**

Use cubes. Show 2 + 5 and 5 + 2.

Solve both problems. Explain how the problems are alike and how they are different.

Activity

### Lesson 1-1
**Addition Fact Strategies**

**I can ...**
count on to add and add in any order.

© **Content Standard** 2.OA.B.2
**Mathematical Practices** MP.2, MP.4, MP.8

$$5 + 2 = 7$$

$$2 + 5 = 7$$

You can count on to find 6 + 3.

6    7   8   9

Or count on to find 3 + 6.

3   4   5   6   7   8   9

*Counting on from the greater number is easier!*

An **equation** uses an equal sign (=) to show that the value on the left is the same as the value on the right.

$$6 + 3 = 9$$

$$3 + 6 = 9$$

You can change the order of the **addends**.

$$6 \quad + \quad 3 \quad = \quad 9$$

$$3 \quad + \quad 6 \quad = \quad 9$$

*The sum is the same.*

addend   addend   **sum**

You can add numbers in any order, and the sum is the same.

So, 6 + 3 = 3 + 6.

You can write the facts this way, too.

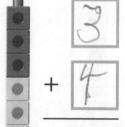

$$\begin{array}{r} 6 \\ + 3 \\ \hline 9 \end{array} \qquad \begin{array}{r} 3 \\ + 6 \\ \hline 9 \end{array}$$

---

**Convince Me!** Does
5 + 2 = 2 + 5?
How do you know?

☆ **Guided Practice** ☆   Count on to find the sum. Then change the order of the addends.

1. 

$$3 + 1 = \underline{4}$$

$$\underline{1} + \underline{3} = \underline{4}$$

2.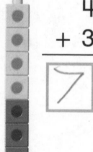

$$\begin{array}{r} 4 \\ + 3 \\ \hline 7 \end{array}$$

$$\begin{array}{r} 3 \\ + 4 \\ \hline 7 \end{array}$$

**Topic 1 | Lesson 1**

**Independent Practice**

Count on to find the sum. Then change the order of the addends. Use cubes if needed.

3.  $8 + 2 = \underline{10}$

$\underline{2} + \underline{8} = \underline{10}$

4.  $8 + 5 = \underline{13}$

$\underline{5} + \underline{8} = \underline{13}$

5.  $9 + 3 = \underline{12}$

$\underline{3} + \underline{9} = \underline{12}$

6.  $8 + 7 = \underline{15}$

$\underline{7} + \underline{8} = \underline{15}$

7.  $7 + 10 = \underline{17}$

$\underline{10} + \underline{7} = \underline{17}$

8.  $7 + 9 = \underline{16}$

$\underline{9} + \underline{7} = \underline{16}$

9.
$$\begin{array}{r} 7 \\ + 2 \\ \hline 9 \end{array}$$

$$\begin{array}{r} \boxed{2} \\ + \boxed{7} \\ \hline \boxed{9} \end{array}$$

10.
$$\begin{array}{r} 6 \\ + 2 \\ \hline \boxed{8} \end{array}$$

$$\begin{array}{r} \boxed{2} \\ + \boxed{6} \\ \hline \boxed{8} \end{array}$$

11.
$$\begin{array}{r} 5 \\ + 6 \\ \hline \boxed{11} \end{array}$$

$$\begin{array}{r} \boxed{6} \\ + \boxed{5} \\ \hline \boxed{11} \end{array}$$

12. **Algebra** Write the missing numbers.

$6 + \underline{4} = 4 + 6$

$8 + 2 = \underline{2} + 8$

$6 + \underline{5} = 5 + 6$

$\underline{4} + 7 = 7 + 4$

$9 + 3 = 3 + \underline{9}$

$\underline{4} + 8 = 8 + 4$

13. **Model** Joy has 8 bean plants and 6 corn plants in her garden. How many plants does she have in all? Draw a picture to explain your thinking. Then write facts for this story with the addends in a different order.

Your picture and your equations will show the problem.

___ + ___ = ___

___ + ___ = ___

14. **Higher Order Thinking** Find the objects in Box 1 and Box 2 that are the same. Write an equation to show how many of each object there are. Then change the order of the addends.

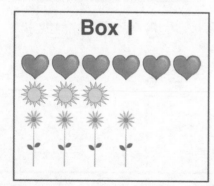

| Box 1 | Box 2 |
|-------|-------|

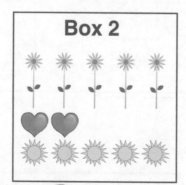

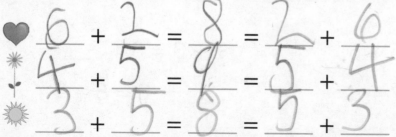

$6 + 2 = 8 = 2 + 6$

$4 + 5 = 9 = 5 + 4$

$3 + 5 = 8 = 5 + 3$

15. ☑ **Assessment Practice** Which shows how to count on to find $7 + 5$?

Ⓐ 7 . . . 8, 9, 10, 11, 12

Ⓑ 1, 2, 3, 4, 5

Ⓒ 7 − 5

Ⓓ 7 . . . 8, 9, 10, 11

Name _____

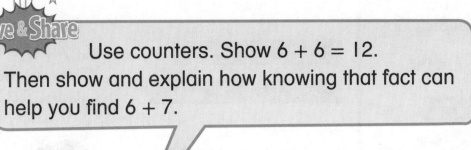

Use counters. Show 6 + 6 = 12.
Then show and explain how knowing that fact can help you find 6 + 7.

**I can ...**
use doubles and near doubles to add quickly and accurately.

© **Content Standard** 2.OA.B.2
**Mathematical Practices** MP.4, MP.6, MP.7

$6 + 6 = 12$

$6 + 7 = 13$

Find 7 + 8 and find 7 + 9.

You can use a doubles fact to help you add.

**Doubles**

3 + 3    5 + 5    4 + 4

You can use the doubles fact to help find a **near doubles** fact.

Doubles Fact: 7 + 7 = 14

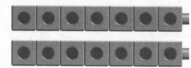

7 + 8 is 1 more than 7 + 7.

7 + 9 is 2 more than 7 + 7.

7 + 8 = 15 and 7 + 9 = 16. These are near doubles facts.

**Convince Me!** How could you use the doubles fact 7 + 7 to find 7 + 9?

☆ **Guided Practice** ☆    Complete the doubles facts. Use the doubles facts to solve the near doubles. Use cubes if needed.

1. 2 + 2 = __4__          2 + 3 = __5__

2. __8__ = 4 + 4          __9__ = 4 + 5

3.  3        3
   + 3      + 4
   ____     ____
   [6]      [7]

4.  5        5
   + 5      + 7
   ____     ____
   [10]     [12]

Activity

## Lesson 1-3
### Make a 10 to Add

**Solve & Share**

How can thinking about 10 help you find 9 + 3?
Use the ten-frames and counters to show how.

### I can …
make a 10 to help me add quickly and accurately.

© **Content Standard** 2.OA.B.2
**Mathematical Practices** MP.1, MP.2, MP.7

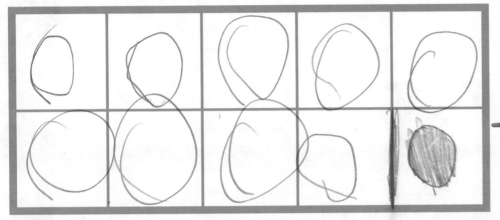

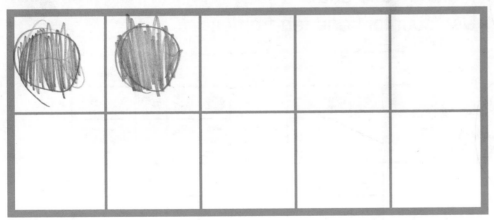

$$\begin{array}{r} 9 \\ +\ 3 \\ \hline 12 \end{array}$$

You can make a 10 to help you add.

$$8 + 5 = \boxed{?}$$

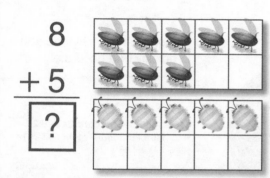

Move 2 counters to make a 10.

Add with 10.

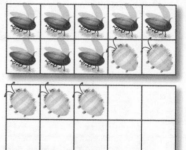

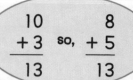

$$\begin{array}{r} 10 \\ + 3 \\ \hline 13 \end{array} \quad \text{so,} \quad \begin{array}{r} 8 \\ + 5 \\ \hline 13 \end{array}$$

**Convince Me!** Why do you move 2 counters to add 8 + 5?

**Guided Practice** ☆ Make a 10 to add.
Use counters and ten-frames.

1. $$\begin{array}{r} 7 \\ + 4 \\ \hline \boxed{?} \end{array}$$

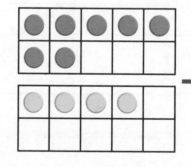 →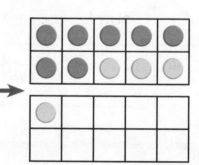

$$\begin{array}{r} 10 \\ + \boxed{|} \\ \hline \boxed{||} \end{array} \quad \text{so,} \quad \begin{array}{r} 7 \\ + \boxed{\phantom{0}} \\ \hline \boxed{\phantom{0}} \end{array}$$

**Topic 1** | Lesson 3

Name _____

Solve & Share

Look at the sums on an addition facts table for addends 0 to 5. Describe one of the patterns that you see.

Use words, colors, or addition facts to describe the patterns.

**I can ...**
use the patterns on an addition facts table to help me remember the addition facts.

 **Content Standard** 2.OA.B.2
**Mathematical Practices** MP.2, MP.7, MP.8

| + | 0 | 1 | 2 | 3 | 4 | 5 |
|---|---|---|---|---|---|---|
| **0** | 0 | 1 | 2 | 3 | 4 | 5 |
| **1** | 1 | 2 | 3 | 4 | 5 | 6 |
| **2** | 2 | 3 | 4 | 5 | 6 | 7 |
| **3** | 3 | 4 | 5 | 6 | 7 | 8 |
| **4** | 4 | 5 | 6 | 7 | 8 | 9 |
| **5** | 5 | 6 | 7 | 8 | 9 | 10 |

_____

_____

_____

_____

How can you describe a pattern for all the sums of six?

It makes a diagonal pattern.

| + | 0 | 1 | 2 | 3 | 4 | 5 | 6 | 7 | 8 | 9 | 10 |
|---|---|---|---|---|---|---|---|---|---|---|----|
| 0 | 0 | 1 | 2 | 3 | 4 | 5 | 6 | 7 | 8 | 9 | 10 |
| 1 | 1 | 2 | 3 | 4 | 5 | 6 | 7 | 8 | 9 | 10 | 11 |
| 2 | 2 | 3 | 4 | 5 | 6 | 7 | 8 | 9 | 10 | 11 | 12 |
| 3 | 3 | 4 | 5 | 6 | 7 | 8 | 9 | 10 | 11 | 12 | 13 |
| 4 | 4 | 5 | 6 | 7 | 8 | 9 | 10 | 11 | 12 | 13 | 14 |
| 5 | 5 | 6 | 7 | 8 | 9 | 10 | 11 | 12 | 13 | 14 | 15 |
| 6 | 6 | 7 | 8 | 9 | 10 | 11 | 12 | 13 | 14 | 15 | 16 |
| 7 | 7 | 8 | 9 | 10 | 11 | 12 | 13 | 14 | 15 | 16 | 17 |
| 8 | 8 | 9 | 10 | 11 | 12 | 13 | 14 | 15 | 16 | 17 | 18 |
| 9 | 9 | 10 | 11 | 12 | 13 | 14 | 15 | 16 | 17 | 18 | 19 |
| 10 | 10 | 11 | 12 | 13 | 14 | 15 | 16 | 17 | 18 | 19 | 20 |

You can write an addition equation.

$4 + 2 = 6$

4 and 2 are addends for the sum of 6.

| + | 0 | 1 | 2 | 3 | 4 |
|---|---|---|---|---|---|
| 0 | 0 | 1 | 2 | 3 | 4 |
| 1 | 1 | 2 | 3 | 4 | 5 |
| 2 | 2 | 3 | 4 | 5 | 6 |

Here are all the ways to make a sum of 6.

$6 + 0 = 6$
$5 + 1 = 6$
$4 + 2 = 6$
$3 + 3 = 6$
$2 + 4 = 6$
$1 + 5 = 6$
$0 + 6 = 6$

What pattern do you see?

**Convince Me!** How can patterns on an addition facts table help you remember the addition facts? Explain.

**Guided Practice** Use fact patterns to complete each equation.

1. $10 + \underline{6} = 16$
   $9 + 7 = \underline{16}$
   $\underline{8} + 8 = 16$
   $7 + \underline{9} = 16$
   $6 + \underline{10} = 16$

2. $10 + \underline{4} = 14$
   $\underline{9} + 5 = 14$
   $8 + 6 = \underline{14}$
   $7 + \underline{7} = 14$
   $\underline{6} + 8 = 14$
   $5 + \underline{9} = 14$
   $\underline{4} + 10 = 14$

3. $9 + \underline{0} = 9$
   $\underline{8} + 1 = 9$
   $7 + 2 = \underline{9}$
   $6 + \underline{3} = 9$
   $\underline{5} + 4 = 9$
   $5 + \underline{4} = 9$
   $\underline{6} + 3 = 9$
   $\underline{7} + 2 = 9$
   $8 + 1 = \underline{9}$
   $\underline{9} + 0 = 9$

Name _____

**Solve & Share**

How can counting help you find 12 – 4? Use the number line to show your work.

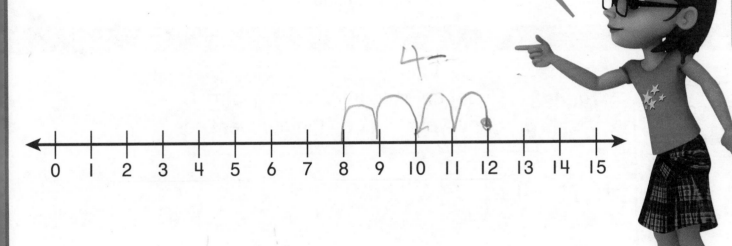

$$12 - 4 = 8$$

Find 10 − 4.   Start with the lesser number.

Count on to 10 to find the **difference**.

You can also count back to subtract.

Start with the greater number.

Count back 4 moves.

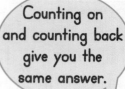

You can count on to subtract.

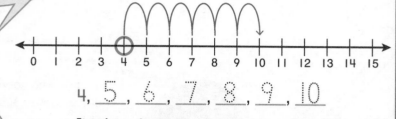

4, _5_, _6_, _7_, _8_, _9_, _10_

It takes 6 moves to count on from 4 to 10.

So, 10 − 4 = 6.

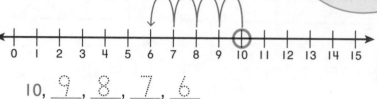

10, _9_, _8_, _7_, _6_

You land on 6. So, 10 − 4 = 6.

Counting on and counting back give you the same answer.

Draw each move as you count.

**Convince Me!** How can you count back on a number line to find 9 − 5?

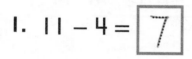

**Guided Practice**  Count on or count back to subtract. Show your work on the number line.

1. 11 − 4 = 7

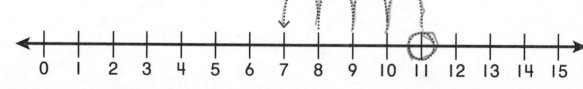

2. 14 − 7 = 7

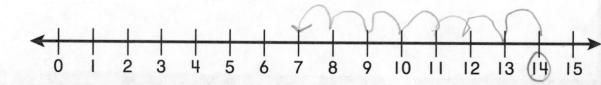

**Topic 1 | Lesson 5**

Name _____

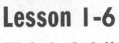

**Solve & Share**

How can you use an addition fact to find 14 – 6? Use counters to help show how.

**I can ...**
use addition to help me subtract quickly and accurately.

**Content Standard** 2.OA.B.2
**Mathematical Practices** MP.2, MP.7, MP.8

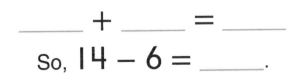

_____ + _____ = _____

So, 14 – 6 = _____.

Find 15 − 7.

One way to subtract is to think about addition.

To find 15 − 7, you can think:

7 plus how many more is 15?
or
7 + ___ = 15

The missing number is the same in both equations.

7 + ___ = 15

15 − 7 = ___

You know the addition fact.

7 + _8_ = 15

You also know the subtraction fact.

15 − 7 = _8_

**Convince Me!** How do you know which addition fact to use to complete the subtraction fact?

★ **Guided Practice**   Think addition to help you subtract.

**1.** 6 − 4 = ?

4 + _2_ = 6

So, 6 − 4 = _2_.

**2.** 9 − 3 = ?

3 + ___ = 9

So, 9 − 3 = ___.

**3.** 14 − 5 = ?

5 + ___ = 14

So, 14 − 5 = ___.

**4.** 12 − 4 = ?

4 + ___ = 12

So, 12 − 4 = ___.

Name _____

**Solve & Share**

14 ladybugs are on a leaf. 6 ladybugs fly away. How can thinking about 10 help you find how many ladybugs are left? Explain.

**I can ...**
make a 10 to help me subtract quickly and accurately.

© **Content Standard** 2.OA.B.2
**Mathematical Practices** MP.3, MP.4, MP.5

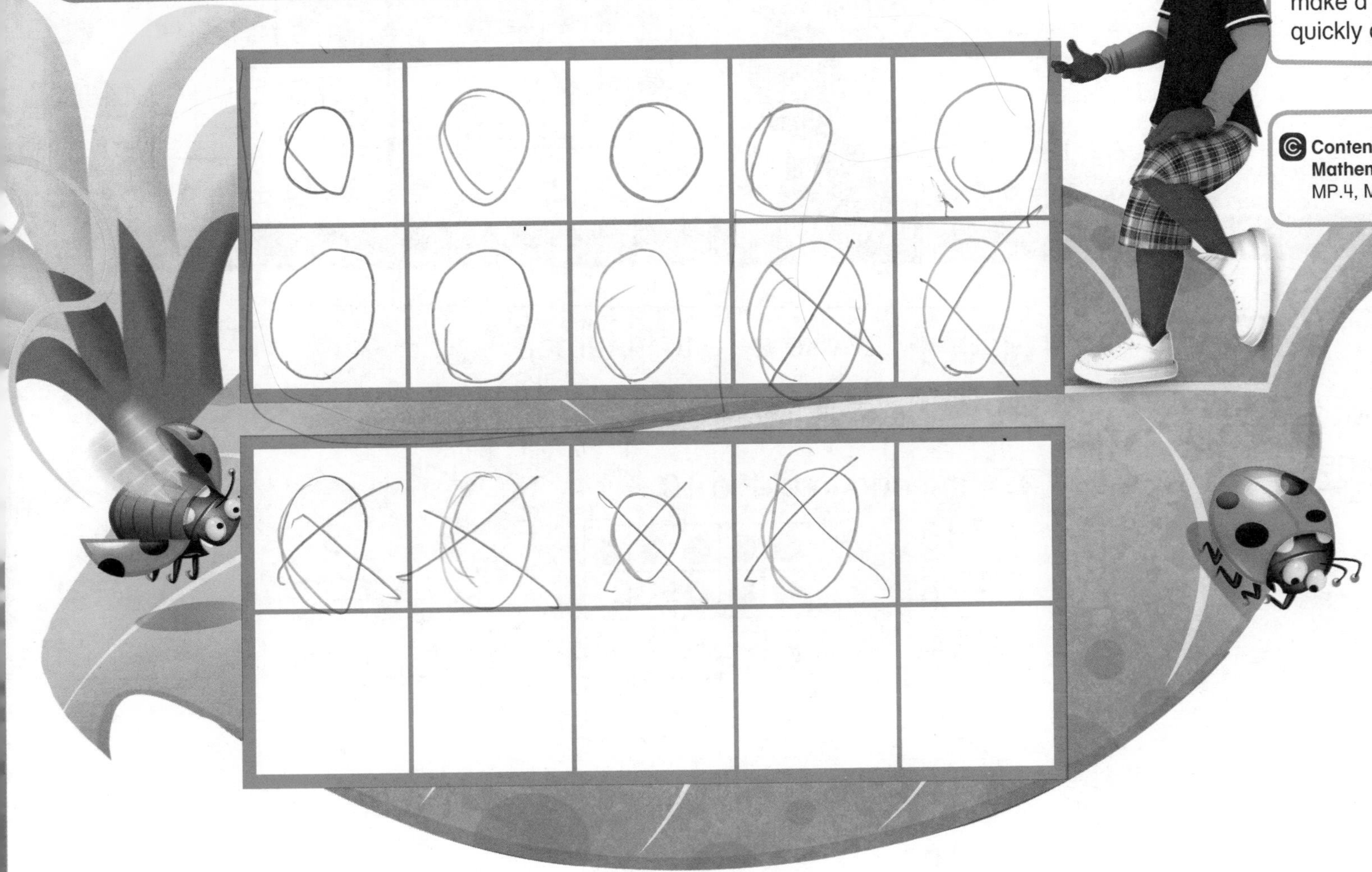

14 ⊖ 6 = 8

Find 13 – 7. You can use 10 to help you subtract.

**One way** is to start with 7 and add 3 to get to 10.

$7 + 3 = 10$

Next, add 3 more to make 13.

$10 + 3 = 13$

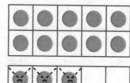
I added 6 to 7 to make 13.

$7 + 6 = 13$,
so $13 - 7 = 6$.

**Another way** is to start with 13 and subtract 3 to get to 10.

$13 - 3 = 10$

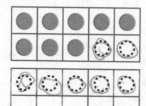

Since $3 + 4 = 7$, subtract 4 more.

$10 - 4 = 6$

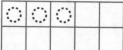

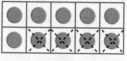
I subtracted 7 and have 6 left.

So, $13 - 7 = 6$.

---

**Convince Me!** Do you prefer to add first to get to 10 or subtract first to get to 10? Explain.

☆ **Guided Practice** ☆   Make a 10 to subtract.
Use counters and your workmat.

1. First add to get to 10.

$$\begin{array}{r} 15 \\ -\ 8 \\ \hline 7 \end{array}$$

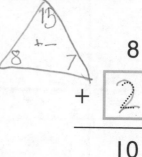

$$\begin{array}{r} 8 \\ +\ 2 \\ \hline 10 \end{array}\qquad \begin{array}{r} 10 \\ +\ 5 \\ \hline 15 \end{array}$$

2. First subtract to get to 10.

$$\begin{array}{r} 16 \\ -\ 7 \\ \hline 9 \end{array}$$

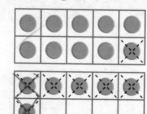

$$\begin{array}{r} 16 \\ -\ 6 \\ \hline 10 \end{array}\qquad \begin{array}{r} 10 \\ -\ 1 \\ \hline 9 \end{array}$$

## Practice Addition and Subtraction Facts

**Solve & Share**

Write four related facts that use both the numbers 7 and 9 as quickly as you can. Hold up your hand when you are done. Then, tell how you found each fact.

**I can ...**
add and subtract quickly and accurately using mental math strategies.

© **Content Standard** 2.OA.B.2
**Mathematical Practices** MP.2, MP.4, MP.8

$$7 + 9 = 16$$
$$9 + 7 = 16$$
$$16 - 7 = 9$$
$$16 - 9 = 7$$

(triangle fact family: 16, +, −, 9, 7)

Practice your basic facts to recall them quickly.

Find 7 − 4.

Think of strategies to help you practice the facts.

One way to subtract is to think about addition.

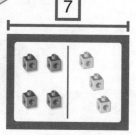

7

$4 + \boxed{3} = 7$

So, $7 − 4 = \boxed{3}$.

Knowing doubles facts can help, too! Find 4 + 5.

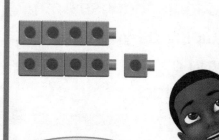

4 + 4 and 1

$4 + 5 = \boxed{9}$

Practicing my basic facts will help me remember the facts quickly. Then my math problems will be easier.

---

**Convince Me!** How can thinking about 10 help you find 14 − 8?

 **Guided Practice**   Add or subtract. Use any strategy.

1. $\begin{array}{r} 14 \\ -\ 9 \\ \hline 5 \end{array}$

2. $\begin{array}{r} 17 \\ -\ 9 \\ \hline 8 \end{array}$

3. $\begin{array}{r} 5 \\ +\ 7 \\ \hline 12 \end{array}$

4. $\begin{array}{r} 10 \\ -\ 5 \\ \hline 5 \end{array}$

5. $\begin{array}{r} 6 \\ -\ 0 \\ \hline 6 \end{array}$

6. $\begin{array}{r} 9 \\ +\ 9 \\ \hline 18 \end{array}$

7. $\begin{array}{r} 12 \\ -\ 4 \\ \hline 8 \end{array}$

8. $\begin{array}{r} 10 \\ +\ 10 \\ \hline 20 \end{array}$

9. $\begin{array}{r} 11 \\ -\ 4 \\ \hline 7 \end{array}$

10. $\begin{array}{r} 9 \\ +\ 1 \\ \hline 10 \end{array}$

11. $\begin{array}{r} 8 \\ +\ 0 \\ \hline 8 \end{array}$

12. $\begin{array}{r} 16 \\ -\ 8 \\ \hline 8 \end{array}$

Name _____

**Solve & Share**

Diego has 6 apples. Leslie has 9 apples.
How many more apples does Leslie have than Diego?

Will you add or subtract to solve this problem? Explain.

## Lesson 1-9

**Solve Addition
and Subtraction
Word Problems**

**I can ...**
use addition and subtraction
to solve word problems.

© **Content Standards** 2.OA.A.1
Also 2.OA.B.2
**Mathematical Practices** MP.1,
MP.2, MP.6

+ −

9        6        3

add    subtract    9 ⊖ 6 ⊖ 3
                        3
Leslie has ___ more apples than Diego.

17 books are on a table. 8 books are on a shelf. How many fewer books are on the shelf than on the table?

You can use a bar diagram and an equation to model the problem.

The shelf has fewer books.

books on table

| 17 |
|---|

| 8 | ? |
|---|---|

books on shelf        fewer books on shelf

You can write an addition or subtraction equation for the problem.

$17 - 8 = \underline{9}$

$8 + \underline{9} = 17$

| 17 |
|---|

| 8 | 9 |
|---|---|

So, there are 9 fewer books on the shelf.

**Convince Me!** Why can you use addition OR subtraction to solve the problem above?

**Guided Practice** Write an equation to solve each problem. Use any strategy.

1. Sam has 5 red tomatoes and 3 green tomatoes. How many tomatoes does he have in all?

$5 \oplus 3 \ominus 8$     __8__ tomatoes

2. There are 16 party hats in a box. There are 10 party hats in a bag. How many fewer hats are in the bag than in the box?

$16 \ominus 10 \ominus 6$     __6__ fewer hats

**Topic 1 | Lesson 9**

Name _____

**Solve & Share**

How can you use the **make a 10** strategy to find 7 + 9?

Explain your thinking and work.
Use pictures, numbers, or words.

**I can ...**
use pictures, numbers, and words to explain why my thinking and work are correct.

Mathematical Practices MP.3
Also MP.1, MP.2, MP.4
**Content Standards** 2.OA.A.1
Also 2.OA.B.2

**Thinking Habits**

How can I use math to explain why my work is correct?

Is my explanation clear?

_____

_____

_____

_____

Does 1 more than 6 + 6 have the same sum as 6 + 7?

Make a math argument.

**How can I make a math argument and show my work?**

I can use pictures, words, or numbers to make a math argument and to show my work.

I can draw pictures and write equations.

6 + 6 = 12

6 + 6 + 1 = 6 + 7

6 + 6 + 1 = 13

6 + 7 = 13

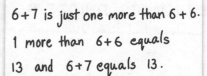

Or I can use words and numbers to make my math argument. My argument is clear and makes sense.

6 + 7 is just one more than 6 + 6.
1 more than 6 + 6 equals
13 and 6 + 7 equals 13.

**Convince Me!** Are both math arguments above clear and complete? Explain.

☆ **Guided Practice** ☆ Use the picture to help you solve the problem. Then use words and numbers to make a math argument.

**1.** Is the sum of 9 + 5 the same as the sum of 10 + 4?

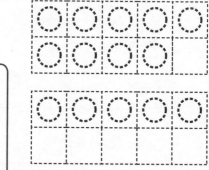

## Independent Practice
Solve each problem. Use words, pictures, and numbers to make a math argument.

2. Lynn had 14 grapes. She ate 8 of them. She wants to eat 6 more grapes. Will Lynn have enough grapes? Explain.

3. The Lions scored 11 runs in a baseball game. The Tigers scored 7 runs. Did the Tigers score 3 fewer runs than the Lions? Explain.

4. Complete the explanation below for how to find 8 + 9. Use pictures, words, or numbers to complete the explanation.

   I Know that 8 + 8 = 16.

### Puppies Sold

The Sunset Pet Store sells puppies. The table shows how many puppies were sold Monday through Thursday.

Is the total number of puppies sold on Tuesday and Wednesday less than the number of puppies sold on Monday?

| Number of Puppies Sold | | | |
|---|---|---|---|
| Monday | Tuesday | Wednesday | Thursday |
| 16 | 10 | 7 | 15 |

5. **Make Sense** Will you use all the numbers in the table to solve the problem? Explain.

_____

_____

_____

6. **Model** Write an equation to find the total number of puppies sold on Tuesday and Wednesday. Solve.

_____

_____

_____

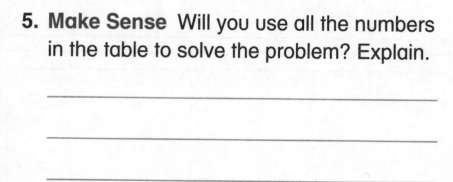

7. **Explain** Solve the problem. Use words, pictures, and numbers to explain your work and thinking.

_____

Name _____

**Find a Match**

Find a partner. Point to a clue. Read the clue.

Look below the clues to find a match. Write the clue letter in the box next to the match.

Find a match for every clue.

**I can ...**
add and subtract within 20.

© **Content Standard** 2.OA.B.2
**Mathematical Practices** MP.3, MP.6, MP.7, MP.8

**Clues**

**A** Near doubles with sums near 8

**B** Every difference is 6.

**C** Ways to make 12

**D** Exactly two differences equal 9.

**E** Every sum is greater than 14.

**F** Exactly three differences are equal.

**G** Near doubles with sums near 6

**H** Every difference equals $14 - 7$.

| | | | |
|---|---|---|---|
| $5 + 7$ <br> $6 + 6$ <br> $8 + 4$ <br> $9 + 3$ | $10 - 5$ <br> $11 - 7$ <br> $12 - 7$ <br> $13 - 8$ | $11 - 5$ <br> $10 - 4$ <br> $12 - 6$ <br> $9 - 3$ | $4 + 3$ <br> $3 + 2$ <br> $2 + 3$ <br> $3 + 4$ |
| $13 - 3$ <br> $9 - 0$ <br> $14 - 6$ <br> $16 - 7$ | $3 + 4$ <br> $5 + 4$ <br> $4 + 3$ <br> $4 + 5$ | $8 + 9$ <br> $7 + 8$ <br> $8 + 7$ <br> $6 + 9$ | $9 - 2$ <br> $13 - 6$ <br> $8 - 1$ <br> $15 - 8$ |

**A-Z**
Glossary

**Word List**
- addend
- bar diagram
- difference
- doubles
- equation
- near doubles
- sum

## Understand Vocabulary

**1.** Circle a doubles fact.

$$\boxed{7 + 7 = 14}$$
$$6 + 7 = 13$$
$$7 + 0 = 7$$

**2.** Circle a near doubles fact.

$$4 + 4 = 8$$
$$4 + 1 = 5$$
$$\boxed{4 + 5 = 9}$$

**3.** Write a subtraction equation using numbers and symbols.

$8 - 2 = 6$

**4.** Find the sum of $8 + 6$.

$14$

**5.** Find the difference of $12 - 5$.

$7$

## Use Vocabulary in Writing

**6.** Describe how you can make a 10 to add $7 + 4$. Use a term from the Word List.

The answer is 11 because $7+3=10$   $10+1=11$

Name _____

**Set A**

You can count on to find a sum.

4    5  6

2  3  4  5  6

I can add numbers in any order and get the same sum.

$4 + 2 = \underline{6}$

$\underline{2} + \underline{4} = \underline{6}$

$4 + 2 = \underline{2} + \underline{4}$

**Reteaching**

Count on to find the sum. Then change the order of the addends.

1.  $9 + 3 = \underline{12}$

    $\underline{3} + \underline{9} = \underline{12}$

    $9 + 3 = \underline{3} + \underline{9}$

2.  $6 + 4 = \underline{10}$

    $\underline{4} + \underline{6} = \underline{10}$

    $6 + 4 = \underline{4} + \underline{6}$

**Set B**

You can use doubles to help you add a near double.

$4 + 4 = \underline{8}$

So, $3 + 4 = \underline{7}$.

3 + 4 is one less than 4 + 4.

So, $3 + 4 = 7$.

Complete the doubles facts. Use the doubles facts to solve the near doubles.

3.    $8 + 8 = \underline{16}$

    So, $7 + 8 = \underline{15}$.

4.    $5 + 5 = \underline{10}$

    So, $6 + 5 = \underline{11}$.

You can make a 10 to help you add $8 + 6$.

$$8 + 6 = ?$$

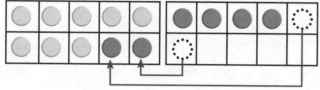

$10 + \underline{4} = \underline{14}$

So, $8 + 6 = \underline{14}$.

Make a 10 to add.

5. $8 + 4 = ?$

10       8

$+ \boxed{2}$    so,    $\underline{+\ 4}$

$\boxed{12}$        $\boxed{12}$

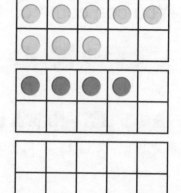

You can count on or count back to find $11 - 4$.

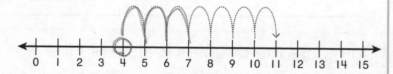

Start at 4 and count on 7 places to 11.

$4 \ldots \underline{5}, \underline{6}, \underline{7}, \underline{8}, \underline{9}, \underline{10}, \underline{11}$     So, $11 - 4 = 7$.

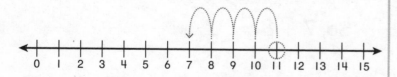

Start at 11 and count back 4 places to get to 7.

$11 \ldots \underline{10}, 9, 8, 7$     So, $11 - 4 = \underline{7}$.

Count on or count back to subtract.
Show your work on the number line.

6. $8 - 5 = \boxed{\phantom{0}}$

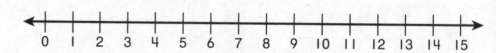

7. $15 - 6 = \boxed{\phantom{0}}$

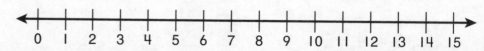

**Set E**

You can think addition to help you subtract.

Find: $16 - 9 = ?$

Think: $9 + \underline{7} = 16$

So, $16 - 9 = \underline{7}$.

Subtract. Write the addition fact that helped you.

**Reteaching**
Continued

8. $13 - 7 = \underline{6}$

$7 + \underline{6} = 13$

9. $17 - 9 = \underline{8}$

$9 + \underline{8} = 17$

**Set F**

You can make a 10 to subtract.
Find $17 - 8$.

Make a 10 to find $13 - 8$.
Draw counters to show your work.

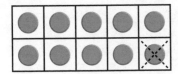

$17 - 7 = 10$

$10 - 1 = 9$

$17 - 8 = \boxed{9}$

10.

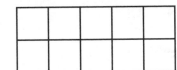

$13 - \underline{3} = 10$

$10 - \underline{3} = \underline{7}$

$13 - 8 = \underline{5}$

You can use addition or subtraction to solve word problems.

11 grapes are in a bowl.
9 grapes are in a cup.
How many fewer grapes are in the cup?

$$11 - 9 = 2 \qquad 9 + 2 = 11$$

So, 2 fewer grapes are in the cup.

---

**Write an equation to solve each problem.**

**11.** 13 shirts are in a closet.
8 shirts are in a box.
How many more shirts are in the closet?

13 ⊕ 8 ⊖ 2 ___ more shirts

**12.** Drake has 10 more books than Yuri.
Yuri has 10 books.
How many books does Drake have?

10 ⊖ 0 ⊖ 10 ___ books

---

**Thinking Habits**

**Construct Arguments**

How can I use math to explain why my work is correct?

Did I use the correct numbers and symbols?

---

**Solve. Use words, pictures, or numbers to construct arguments.**

**13.** Tyler read 15 pages of a book.
Ann read 9 pages of the same book.
Did Tyler read 4 more pages than Ann? Explain.

Name _____

## Farm Kittens

Many kittens are born each summer at the Sunshine Farm. The table shows the number of kittens born at the farm from June to August.

| Number of Kittens Born | | |
|:---:|:---:|:---:|
| June | July | August |
| 13 | 8 | 7 |

**2.** Write an equation to find the total number of kittens born in July and August. Solve.

_____

_____

_____

_____

_____

**1.** During which two months were a total of 20 kittens born?

**3.** Joy said 5 more kittens were born in June than in August. Do you agree? Circle Yes or No.

Show your work to explain.

Yes          No

**4.** Use the clues to complete the table below.

- No kittens were born in December, January, and February.

- In March, 6 kittens were born.

- Three kittens were born in April and in September.

- In May, 4 kittens were born.

- Two kittens were born in October and in November.

| Kittens Born at the Sunshine Farm | | |
|---|---|---|
| Season | Months | Number of Kittens Born |
| Spring | March, April, and May | |
| Summer | June, July, and August | 28 |
| Fall | September, October, and November | |
| Winter | December, January, and February | |

**5.** Joy says that more kittens were born in the summer than in all other seasons combined. Is she correct? Explain.

_____

_____

_____

_____

_____

**6.** How many more kittens were born in the spring than in the fall?

Show how to solve the problem with a subtraction equation.

# Work with Equal Groups

**Essential Questions:** How can you show even and odd numbers?
How do arrays relate to repeated addition?

**Digital Resources**

Interactive Student Edition · Activity · Visual Learning · Video · Practice

Assessment · Games · Tools · Glossary

Look at these plants and animals!

What plants and animals live in your area?

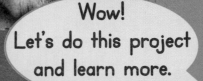

Wow! Let's do this project and learn more.

## ēnVision® STEM Project: Plants, Animals, and Arrays

**Find Out** Make lists of different types of plants and wild animals that you see. Look in your neighborhood or in a nearby park. Look at how the animals and plants come together.

**Journal: Make a Book** Show what you find out in a book. In your book, also:

• Tell about plants or animals that you see in groups. Look for patterns.

• Make an array of a group of plants and an array of a group of animals.

Name _____

# Review What You Know

## A-Z Vocabulary

**1.** Circle the **addends** in the math below.

$5 + 8 = 13$

$8 - 5 = 3$

**2.** Complete the **sum** in the **equation** below.

$5 + 7 =$ _____

**3.** Write the **doubles** fact that the model shows.

## Near Doubles

**4.** Find each sum.

$7 + 6 =$ _____

$4 + 5 =$ _____

$9 + 8 =$ _____

## Add in Any Order

**5.** Change the order of the addends and complete both equations.

$6 + 8 =$ _____

_____ $+$ _____ $=$ _____

## Math Story

**6.** Five brown cows go into the barn. Then 8 black and white cows go into the barn. How many cows are now in the barn?

_____ cows

Name _____

**PROJECT
2A**

## What kinds of birds live near you?

**Project:** Collect Bird Data

**PROJECT
2B**

## What are scutes?

**Project:** Make a Scutes Poster

### PROJECT 2C

# How can you arrange trees in an orchard?

**Project:** Create an Orchard Model

### PROJECT 2D

# How do your flowers grow?

**Project:** Draw a Picture of Flowers

**Topic 2** | Pick a Project

Name _____

Activity

**Solve & Share**

Use cubes to make the numbers below. Shade all the numbers that can be shown as two equal groups of cubes.
What do you notice about the numbers you shaded?

**I can ...**
tell if a group of objects is even or odd.

**Content Standards** 2.OA.C.3 Also 2.OA.B.2
**Mathematical Practices** MP.4, MP.6, MP.7

| 1 | 2 | 3 | 4 | 5 | 6 | 7 | 8 | 9 | 10 |
|---|---|---|---|---|---|---|---|---|----|
| 11 | 12 | 13 | 14 | 15 | 16 | 17 | 18 | 19 | 20 |

Go Online | SavvasRealize.com

sixty-o

62

How can you tell if a number is **even** or **odd**?

Use cubes to find out.

8

9

---

An even number can be shown as two equal parts using cubes.

8 is even.
$4 + 4 = 8$

---

An odd number cannot be shown as two equal parts using cubes.

9 is odd.
$5 + 4 = 9$

---

The ones digit tells you if a number is even or odd.

18 is even.
19 is odd.

| 1 | 2 | 3 | 4 | 5 | 6 | 7 | 8 | 9 | 10 |
|---|---|---|---|---|---|---|---|---|----|
| 11 | 12 | 13 | 14 | 15 | 16 | 17 | 18 | 19 | 20 |

---

**Convince Me!** You break apart a tower of cubes to make two equal parts, but there is one cube left over. Is the number of cubes even or odd? Explain.

**Guided Practice** Look at the number. Circle even or odd. Then write the equation.

1.

14

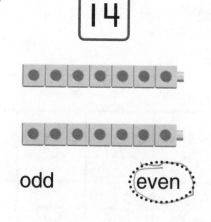

odd (even)

7 + 7 = 14

2.

19

(odd) even

10 + 9 = 19

**Topic 2 | Lesson 1**

Name _____

**Solve & Share**

The students in Ms. Jenn's class work in pairs. One student does not have a partner. How many students could be in Ms. Jenn's class?

Use cubes to show your thinking. Draw a picture of your work.

**I can ...**
use different ways to tell if a group of objects shows an even or odd number.

Content Standards 2.OA.C.3 Also 2.OA.B.2
Mathematical Practices MP.4, MP.7, MP.8

This is odd.

Visual Learning · A-Z Glossary

**What patterns do you see?**

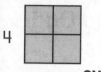

4    6

**even**

3    5

**odd**

Think about pairs of objects and the shape an even number makes.

**If you can count the squares by 2s the number is even.**

**even**

2

**even**

2,  4

**The sum of two equal addends equals an even number.**

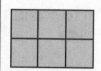

$3 + 3 = 6$

$4 + 4 = 8$

**The pattern in the sums is to skip count by 2s.**

$1 + 1 = 2$

$2 + 2 = 4$

$3 + 3 = 6$

$4 + 4 = 8$

What is the next even number after 8?

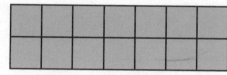

The next even number is 10.

---

**Convince Me!** Is the number 10 even or odd? Draw a picture to show how you know.

**Guided Practice**  Write the number for each model. Circle even or odd. Then write the equation.

1.

7    even    (odd)

$4 + 3 = 7$

2.

14    (even)    odd

$7 + 7 = 14$

Topic 2 | Lesson 2

Name _____

**Solve & Share**

Show and explain two different ways to find how many circles in all.

**I can ...**
find the total number of objects in a set of rows and columns.

© **Content Standards** 2.OA.C.4 Also 2.OA.B.2
**Mathematical Practices** MP.1, MP.3, MP.7

$5 \times 3 = 15$

 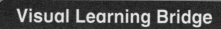
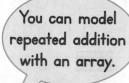

You can model repeated addition with an array.

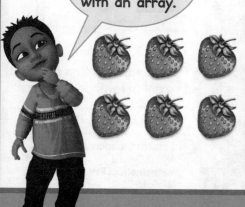

Arrays have equal **rows**. Each row has 3 strawberries.

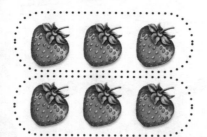

Arrays have equal **columns**. Each column has 2 strawberries.

Write two equations that match the array.

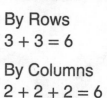 

By Rows
$3 + 3 = 6$

By Columns
$2 + 2 + 2 = 6$

**Convince Me!** Is this group an array? Explain.

☆ **Guided Practice** ☆ Write two equations that match each array.

**1.**

By Rows

$\underline{4} + \underline{4} = \underline{8}$

By Columns

$\underline{2} + \underline{2} + \underline{2} + \underline{2} = \underline{8}$

**2.**

By Rows

$\underline{3} + \underline{3} + \underline{3} = \underline{9}$

By Columns

$\underline{3} + \underline{3} + \underline{3} = \underline{9}$

**Topic 2** | Lesson 3

## Name _____

**Solve & Share**

Rusty places his toy trucks in 4 columns. He places 3 trucks in each column. How many trucks does Rusty have in all?

Show how you know with counters and an equation.

### Lesson 2-4
**Make Arrays to Find Totals**

**I can ...**
make arrays with equal rows or equal columns.

 **Content Standards** 2.OA.C.4
Also 2.OA.B.2
**Mathematical Practices** MP.2, MP.4, MP.5

$9 + 3 = 12$   $\quad$   $4 \times 3 = 12$

**Equation**

$3 + 3 + 3 + 3 = 12$

_12_ trucks

Jackson's garden has 2 rows with 4 carrots in each row.

How many carrots are in his garden?

You can make an array to show the problem.

Use repeated addition to find out how many carrots are in Jackson's garden.

You can add the number of carrots in each row.

$4 + 4 = \underline{8}$

Repeated addition means adding the same number over and over.

You can also add the number of carrots in each column.

$2 + 2 + 2 + 2 = \underline{8}$

$4 + 4 = \underline{8}$

I have 8 carrots!

---

**Convince Me!** If you have 2 rows with a different amount in each row, do you have an array? Explain.

☆ **Guided Practice** ☆ Draw an array to show each problem. Use repeated addition to solve.

1. Monica puts cans of peas in 2 rows with 3 cans in each row.
   How many cans of peas does she have in all?

   $\underline{3} + \underline{3} = \underline{6}$ cans of peas

   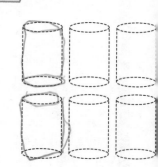

2. Dominick is organizing his stickers in columns. He has 4 columns with 4 stickers in each column. How many stickers does he have in all?

   $\underline{4} + \underline{4} + \underline{4} + \underline{4} = \underline{16}$ stickers

**Topic 2** | Lesson 4

Name _____

**Solve & Share**

There are 4 rows in a classroom. Two rows have 3 tables in each row. Two rows have 4 tables in each row. How many tables are there in all?

Draw a picture and write an equation to model and solve the problem.

**I can ...**
model problems using equations, drawings, and arrays.

© **Mathematical Practices** MP.4
Also MP.1, MP.3, MP.6, MP.7, MP.8
**Content Standards** 2.OA.C.4
Also 2.OA.A.1, 2.OA.B.2

000 6        3+3+4+4=14
006 6
         +
0008
00008
         =
         14

**Thinking Habits**

How can a picture and an equation help me model problems?

Does my answer make sense?

Equation: 3+3+4+4=14  x3=1?

14 tables

Pat makes an array of marbles. The array has 3 rows. She places 5 marbles in each row. How many marbles does Pat have in all?

Use a model to show and solve the problem.

**How can I use a model to show and solve the problem?**

I can draw an array and write an equation to show how many marbles in all.

$5 + 5 + 5 = 15$

So, Pat has 15 marbles.

Or I can draw the same array and write a different equation.

My drawings and equations show that Pat has 15 marbles in all.

$3 + 3 + 3 + 3 + 3 = 15$

So, Pat has 15 marbles.

**Convince Me!** How does drawing a picture and writing an equation help you model a problem?

☆ **Guided Practice** ☆ Draw a picture and write an equation to show each problem. Then solve.

1. Ray has 2 rows of books.
He has 5 books in each row.
How many books does Ray have in all?

$\underline{5} + \underline{5} = \underline{10}$ books

Name _____

Color a path from **Start** to **Finish**. Follow the sums and differences that are odd numbers. You can only move up, down, right, or left.

**I can ...**
add and subtract within 20.

Ⓒ **Content Standard** 2.OA.B.2
**Mathematical Practices** MP.2, MP.6, MP.7

| Start | | | | | | | | |
|---|---|---|---|---|---|---|---|---|
| 5 + 6 | 14 − 6 | 13 − 9 | 7 − 3 | 1 + 9 | 10 − 5 | 2 + 9 | 9 + 8 | 16 − 7 |
| 3 + 4 | 14 − 7 | 2 + 5 | 11 − 6 | 4 + 8 | 8 − 3 | 12 − 6 | 1 + 5 | 11 − 4 |
| 7 − 1 | 4 + 4 | 12 − 4 | 12 − 7 | 14 − 9 | 4 + 7 | 15 − 7 | 2 + 5 | 1 + 8 |
| 9 + 9 | 1 + 7 | 6 − 4 | 2 + 8 | 6 + 2 | 1 + 9 | 13 − 9 | 15 − 6 | 2 + 4 |
| 17 − 9 | 3 + 9 | 7 + 5 | 8 + 8 | 16 − 6 | 9 − 5 | 10 − 6 | 5 + 4 | 10 − 3 |

Finish

A-Z
Glossary

**Word List**
- addends
- array
- column
- doubles
- equation
- even
- odd
- row
- sum

## Understand Vocabulary

Choose a term from the Word List to complete each sentence.

1. An _____ number cannot be shown as pairs of cubes.

2. An _array_ is a group of objects set in equal rows and columns.

3. In an array, objects that are shown across are in a _row_.

4. _addends_ are numbers that are added.

Write T for *true* or F for *false*.

5. _F_ 9 is an even number.

6. _T_ 13 is an odd number.

7. _sum_ You can model repeated addition with an array.

8. _____ In an array, objects that are shown up and down are in a column.

## Use Vocabulary in Writing

9. Which model could you use to show 4 groups of 5 objects in each group?
   Use at least 1 term from the Word List.

Name _____

### Set A

You can use cubes to tell if a number is even or odd.

The number of cubes is even if you can pair or count them by 2s.

$$12$$

odd    (even)

$$6 + 6 = 12$$

Circle even or odd. Then write the equation. Use cubes to help.

1.

$$11$$

(odd)    even

$$5 + 6 = 11$$

2.

$$18$$

odd    (even)

$$9 + 9 = 18$$

### Set B

You can use repeated addition to find the total number of loaves.

Write two equations that match the array.

Rows: $3 + 3 = 6$

Columns: $2 + 2 + 2 = 6$

Write two equations that match the array.

3.

Rows: $5 + 5 + 5 + 5 = 20$

Columns:

$$4 + 4 + 4 + 4 + 4 = 20$$

You can draw arrays and use repeated addition to solve problems.

Alli sets 3 rows of cans in her pantry.
She puts 4 cans of beans in each row.
How many cans of beans does Alli have in all?

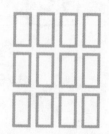

$\underline{4} + \underline{4} + \underline{4} = \underline{12}$ cans

### Thinking Habits

**Model with Math**

Can I use a drawing, array, table, or graph to model the problem?

Can I write an equation to show the problem?

Draw an array to show the problem.
Use repeated addition to solve.

4. Steven puts 3 rows of apples on a table. Each row has 5 apples. How many apples does Steven put on the table?

$\underline{5} + \underline{5} + \underline{5} = \underline{15}$ apples

Draw a model and solve the problem.

5. There are 3 columns of cars.
   Each column has 3 cars.
   How many cars are in the parking lot?

$\underline{3} + \underline{3} + \underline{3} = \underline{9}$ cars

Name _____

1. José writes an equation.
The sum is an even number
greater than 14.

Which equation does José write?

Ⓐ  6 + 6 = 12

Ⓑ  6 + 7 = 13

Ⓒ  8 + 8 = 16

Ⓓ  8 + 7 = 15

2. Jen has 2 rows of apples
with 4 apples in each row.

Which equation shows how
many apples Jen has in all?

Ⓐ  4 + 2 = 6

Ⓑ  2 + 2 + 2 = 6

Ⓒ  4 + 4 = 8

Ⓓ  4 + 4 + 4 = 12

3. Choose Yes or No to tell if the sum in the equation is an even number.

3 + 4 = 7

○ Yes  ○ No

5 + 5 = 10

○ Yes  ○ No

7 + 6 = 13

○ Yes  ○ No

9 + 7 = 16

○ Yes  ○ No

4. Will has 3 rows of trees in his yard.
Each row has 4 trees.
How many trees in all?

Draw a picture to show the array
of trees.

Then write an equation for your
picture.

____ + ____ + ____ = ____

There are ____ trees in all.

**5.** How many squares are shown? Is the number even or odd?

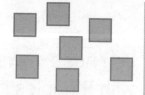

Draw a picture to show how you know.

**6.** Ben has 8 pennies. Look at each equation. Choose Yes or No to tell if Ben can use the equation to make an array with his pennies.

$2 + 2 + 2 + 2 = 8$    ○ Yes   ○ No

$5 + 3 = 8$    ○ Yes   ○ No

$4 + 4 = 8$    ○ Yes   ○ No

$6 + 2 = 8$    ○ Yes   ○ No

**7.** Becky drew this bar diagram to show 2 equal groups can make 14.

**Part A**
Draw a picture to show what the "?" stands for.

**Part B**
Change 14 to 16 in the bar diagram. What does the "?" stand for now? Tell how you know.

Name _____

**Performance Task**

## School Garden
Students are planting a garden at school.
The pictures show the number of some plants
in the garden.

**Number of Tomato Plants**

**Number of Corn Plants**

1. Is there an even or odd
   number of tomato plants
   in the garden?

   Circle your answer.   **even        odd**

   Use the pictures of tomatoes to show how
   you know. Explain your thinking below.

2. Tom says the number of corn plants is an
   even number. Do you agree? Draw a picture
   to show why or why not.

**3.** David plants peas in the school garden. He plants 4 rows of peas with 3 plants in each row.

### Part A

Draw an array to show how David planted the peas.

### Part B

Write an equation to match the array. How many pea plants does David plant?

**4.** Jesse says there are other ways to make an array of 12 plants. Show an array of 12 plants that is different from the array David used.

**5.** The array below shows the number of pepper plants in the garden.

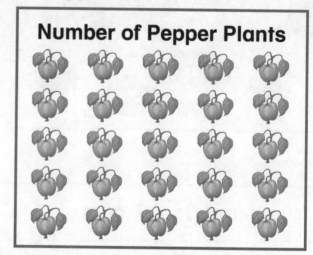

**Number of Pepper Plants**

Add the number of plants in each row. How many pepper plants are in the garden?

____ + ____ + ____ + ____ + ____ = ____

_____ pepper plants

Is the number of pepper plants an even or an odd number?     **even     odd**

# Add Within 100 Using Strategies

**Essential Question:** What are strategies for adding numbers to 100?

**Digital Resources**

Interactive Student Edition | Activity | Visual Learning | Video | Practice

Assessment | Games | Tools | Glossary | A-Z

The Earth is always changing!

Some changes can happen quickly. Others take a long time.

Wow! Let's do this project and learn more.

## enVision® STEM Project: Earth Changes and Addition Strategies

**Find Out** Find and share books about how the Earth changes. Talk about changes that people can see, hear, and feel. Talk about changes that people cannot see happening.

**Journal: Make a Book** Show what you learn in a book. In your book, also:

• Write new science words you learn. Draw pictures that help show what the words mean.

• Write new math words you learn. Draw pictures that help show what the words mean.

Name _____

# Review What You Know

**A-Z Vocabulary**

1. Draw a circle around each **even** number. Use cubes to help.

    15    7    14

    2    19    18

2. Draw a square around each **odd** number. Use cubes to help.

    12    3    6

    17    11    4

3. Complete the **bar diagram** to show the sum of $3 + 5$.

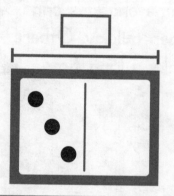

## Arrays

Write an equation to show the number of circles in each array.

4.

By rows

_____ + _____ = _____

5.

By columns

_____ + _____ + _____ = _____

## Math Story

6. Joe has 5 apples. He picks 3 more apples. How many apples does Joe have now?

    _____ apples

    Does Joe have an even or an odd number of apples?

    _____ number

Topic 3

Name _____

**PROJECT 3A**

How far would you travel to cheer for your team?

**Project:** Make a Map to the Game

**PROJECT 3B**

What are some important things to do at the airport?

**Project:** Write a List of Air Travel Tasks

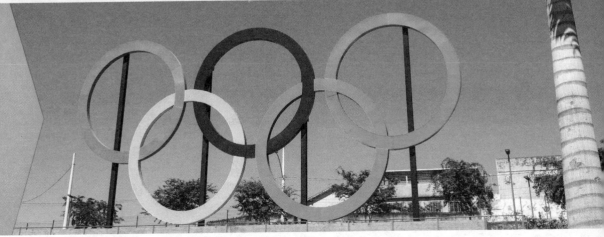

**PROJECT 3C**

How many Olympic Games have there been?

**Project:** Create an Olympics Poster

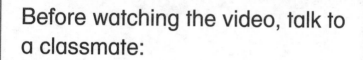

## Math Modeling

## Piled Up

Video

Before watching the video, talk to a classmate:

When you have a large number of items, it's not easy to count them all. What are some strategies you use to speed up the process? How is counting different from adding?

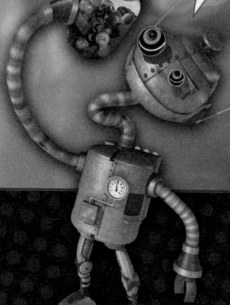

## I can ...

model with math to solve a problem that involves using strategies and make a 10 to add.

© **Mathematical Practices** MP.4 Also MP.7, MP.8
**Content Standards** 2.NBT.B.5 Also 2.OA.A.1, 2.OA.C.4, 2.NBT.B.9

**Solve & Share**

How can you use the hundred chart to help you find 32 + 43? Explain.

Write an equation to show the sum.

**I can ...**
add within 100 using place-value strategies and properties of operations.

© **Content Standards** 2.NBT.B.5 Also 2.NBT.B.9
**Mathematical Practices** MP.3, MP.5

| 1 | 2 | 3 | 4 | 5 | 6 | 7 | 8 | 9 | 10 |
|---|---|---|---|---|---|---|---|---|---|
| 11 | 12 | 13 | 14 | 15 | 16 | 17 | 18 | 19 | 20 |
| 21 | 22 | 23 | 24 | 25 | 26 | 27 | 28 | 29 | 30 |
| 31 | 32 | 33 | 34 | 35 | 36 | 37 | 38 | 39 | 40 |
| 41 | 42 | 43 | 44 | 45 | 46 | 47 | 48 | 49 | 50 |
| 51 | 52 | 53 | 54 | 55 | 56 | 57 | 58 | 59 | 60 |
| 61 | 62 | 63 | 64 | 65 | 66 | 67 | 68 | 69 | 70 |
| 71 | 72 | 73 | 74 | 75 | 76 | 77 | 78 | 79 | 80 |
| 81 | 82 | 83 | 84 | 85 | 86 | 87 | 88 | 89 | 90 |
| 91 | 92 | 93 | 94 | 95 | 96 | 97 | 98 | 99 | 100 |

It is 75 because 30+40=70 and 2+3=5 32+45=75.

$32 + 43 = 75$

You can add on a hundred chart. Find 54 + 18.

**One Way**

Add the tens first.

Start at 54. Add 18.
Move down 1 row to add 1 ten.
Then move ahead 8 to add 8 ones.
54 + 18 = 72

| 51 | 52 | 53 | 54 | 55 | 56 | 57 | 58 | 59 | 60 |
|----|----|----|----|----|----|----|----|----|----|
| 61 | 62 | 63 | 64 | 65 | 66 | 67 | 68 | 69 | 70 |
| 71 | 72 | 73 | 74 | 75 | 76 | 77 | 78 | 79 | 80 |

**Another Way** Add the ones first.

Start at 54. Add 18.
Move ahead 8 to add 8 ones.
Then move down 1 row to add 1 ten.
54 + 18 = 72
I get the same sum both ways!

| 51 | 52 | 53 | 54 | 55 | 56 | 57 | 58 | 59 | 60 |
|----|----|----|----|----|----|----|----|----|----|
| 61 | 62 | 63 | 64 | 65 | 66 | 67 | 68 | 69 | 70 |
| 71 | 72 | 73 | 74 | 75 | 76 | 77 | 78 | 79 | 80 |

**Convince Me!** Max says that to find 54 + 18 on a hundred chart, you can start at 54, move down 2 rows, and move back 2 spaces. Do you agree? Explain.

**✩ Guided Practice ✩** Add using the hundred chart.
Draw arrows on the chart if needed.

| 11 | 12 | 13 | 14 | 15 | 16 | 17 | 18 | 19 | 20 |
|----|----|----|----|----|----|----|----|----|----|
| 21 | 22 | 23 | 24 | 25 | 26 | 27 | 28 | 29 | 30 |
| 31 | 32 | 33 | 34 | 35 | 36 | 37 | 38 | 39 | 40 |
| 41 | 42 | 43 | 44 | 45 | 46 | 47 | 48 | 49 | 50 |

1. 17 + 32 = __49__

2. 28 + 21 = __49__

3. __39__ = 19 + 20

4. 18 + 8 = __26__

Name _____

**Solve & Share**

How can you use the open number line to find
35 + 24?

Write an equation to show the sum. Explain your work.

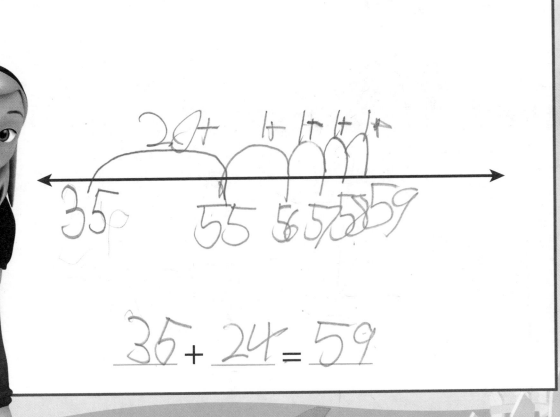

35 + 24 = 59

Find 48 + 23. Use an **open number line**.

**One Way**

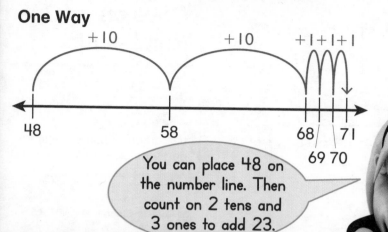

You can place 48 on the number line. Then count on 2 tens and 3 ones to add 23.

**Another Way**

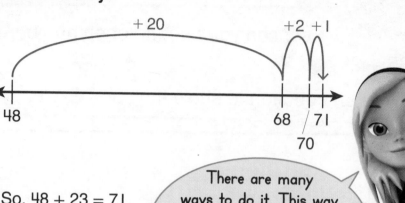

So, 48 + 23 = 71.

There are many ways to do it. This way shows a jump of 20, then 2, then 1 to add 23. Both ways land on 71.

**Convince Me!** Explain how you can use an open number line to find 56 + 35.

 **Guided Practice** Use an open number line to find each sum.

1. 59 + 24 = __83__

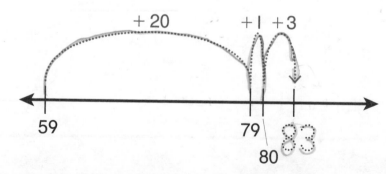

2. 47 + 25 = __72__

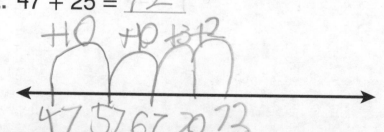

Solve & Share

Josh has 34 cans to recycle. Jill has 27 cans. How many cans do they have in all?

Solve any way you choose. Use drawings and equations to explain your work.

**I can ...**
break apart numbers into tens and ones to find their sum.

Content Standards 2.NBT.B.5 Also 2.NBT.B.9
Mathematical Practices MP.4, MP.7

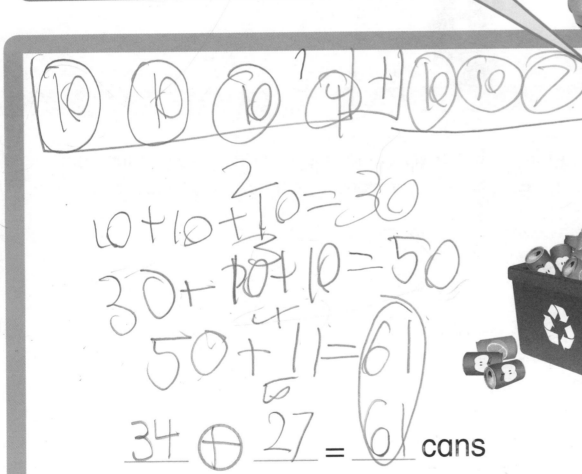

$$10 + 10 + 10 = 30$$
$$30 + 10 + 10 = 50$$
$$50 + 11 = 61$$

$$34 + 27 = 61 \text{ cans}$$

37 + 25 = ?

You can **break apart** just the second addend into **tens** and **ones**.

37     +     25   =   ?

| 37 | 20 | 5 |

25 is 2 tens and 5 ones or 20 + 5.

37 + 25 = 37 + 20 + 5

Start at one addend. Add the **tens** and **ones** of the second addend.

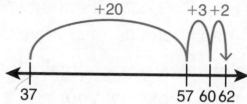
+20     +3 +2

37        57 60 62

37 + **20** = 57

57 + **3** = 60

60 + **2** = 62

So, 37 + 25 = __62__.

**Convince Me!** Explain how you can break apart 28 to find 33 + 28.

☆**Guided**☆ Break apart the second addend to find the sum.
**Practice** Show your work. Use an open number line to help.

1. 57     +     13 = __70__

| 57 | 10 | 3 |

__57__ + __10__ = __67__

__67__ + __3__ = __70__

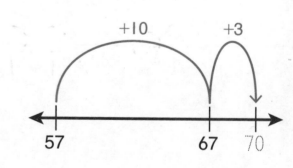
+10     +3

57       67   70

**Topic 3** | Lesson

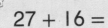 Name _____

**Solve & Share**

27 + 16 = _____

Draw counters on the ten-frames to show each addend.

Then show how you can move some counters to make it easier to find the sum.

Explain your work.

### I can ...
break apart addends and combine them in different ways to make numbers that are easy to add mentally.

**Content Standard** 2.NBT.B.5
**Mathematical Practices** MP.2, MP.3, MP.8

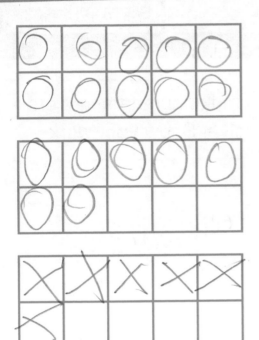

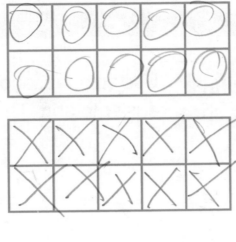

27 + 16 = 43

Find 18 + 15.

There are many ways to use compensation to make numbers that are easier to add.

20    13

**One way** Take 2 from 15 and give it to 18 to make 20.

18 + 15 = ?

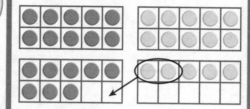

20 + 13 = 33

Show how you changed the numbers to make them easier to add.

18  +  15  = ?
+2      −2

20  +  13

10 + 3

20 + 10 + 3 = 33

So, 20 + 13 = 33.

If you give an amount to one addend, you must take away the same amount from the other addend, so the sum stays the same.

18 + 15 = 20 + 13

So, 18 + 15 = 33.

---

**Convince Me!** Solve.

19 + 26 = ☐

Explain how you can change the addends to make them easier to add.

☆ **Guided Practice** ☆ Use compensation to make numbers that are easier to add. Then solve. Show your work.

+3
1. 17  +  9  = _____

⊕ 3    ⊖ 3

20  +  6  = 26

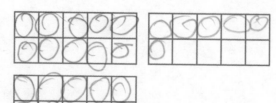

+4
2. 16  +  14  = 30

⊕ 4    ⊖ 4

20  +  10  = 30

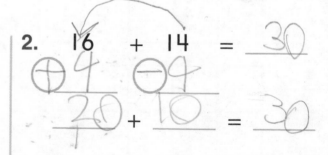

**Topic 3** | Lesson 4

**Lesson 3-5**

**Practice Adding Using Strategies**

I can ...
choose a strategy to help me add two-digit numbers.

© **Content Standards** 2.NBT.B.5 Also 2.NBT.B.9
**Mathematical Practices** MP.2, MP.4

Solve & Share

Tameka has 39 blocks. Kim has 43 blocks. How many blocks do they have in all?

Choose any strategy. Solve. Show and explain your work.

+30      +40

43      73      82  83

40+30=70

3+9=12    70+12=82

____ blocks

Find 66 + 25.

You can break apart numbers or use compensation.

**One Way**

Break apart 25 into tens and ones. Then add.

$$66 + 25$$

$$66 + 20 + 5$$

$$4 + 1$$

$66 + 20 = 86$
$86 + \phantom{0}4 = 90$
$90 + \phantom{0}1 = 91$

**Another Way**

Use compensation to make it easier to find the sum.

$66 + 25 = ?$
$+4$
$70 + 25 = 95 \longrightarrow 91$
$\phantom{70 + 25 = 95}-4$

You get the same answer both ways!

So, $66 + 25 = 91$.

---

**Convince Me!** In 66 + 25 above, why was 4 added to 66 and then subtracted from 95?

☆ **Guided Practice** ☆ Find each sum. Use any strategy. Show your work.

1. $14 + 32 = \underline{46}$

$14 + 30 + 2$

$44 + 2 = 46$

2. $67 + 26 = \underline{\phantom{00}}$

$60 + 20 = 80$

$6 + 7 = 13$

$8 + 10 = 90$

$90 + 3 = 93$

Name _____

**Solve & Share**

The red team has 15 more points than the blue team. The blue team has 36 points. How many points does the red team have?

Choose any strategy. Solve. Explain your work.

**I can ...**
use drawings and equations to solve one-step and two-step problems.

© **Content Standards** 2.OA.A.1 Also 2 NBT.B.5
**Mathematical Practices** MP.1, MP.6

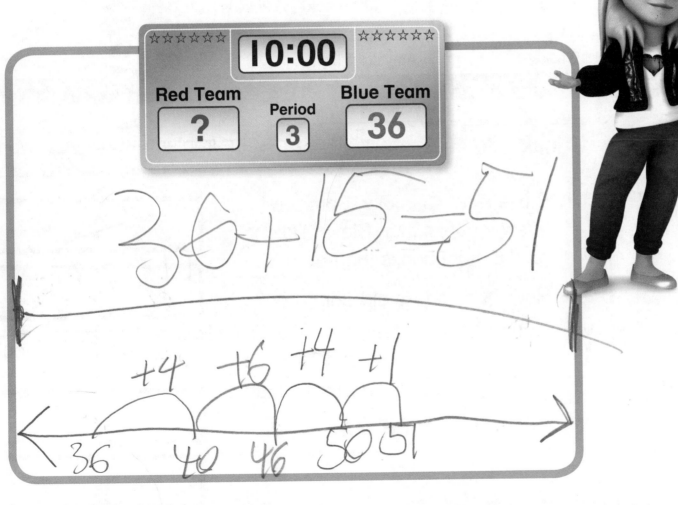

**10:00**

| Red Team | Period | Blue Team |
|:---:|:---:|:---:|
| ? | 3 | 36 |

$$30 + 15 = 51$$

+4   +6   +4   +1

36   40   46   50 51

Matt sold 17 tickets.
Jenn sold 8 fewer tickets than Matt.
Amy sold 3 more tickets than Jenn.

How many tickets did each person sell?

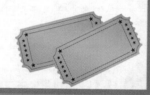

**Step 1**

tickets Matt sold

| 17 |
|----|

| 8 | 9 |
|---|---|

fewer    tickets
tickets    Jenn sold

$17 - 8 = 9$
Jenn sold 9 tickets.

**Step 2**

tickets Amy sold

| 12 |
|----|

| 9 | 3 |
|---|---|

tickets    more
Jenn sold    tickets

$9 + 3 = 12$
Amy sold 12 tickets.

Matt:    17 tickets
Jenn:    9 tickets
Amy:    12 tickets

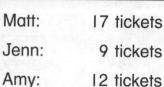

Look back! Does your answer make sense?

**Convince Me!** What steps did you take to find the number of tickets Amy sold? Explain.

**Guided Practice** Solve the two-step problem. Show your work.

1. Steve read 15 books. Sam read 9 fewer books than Steve. Dixon read 8 more books than Sam.

How many books did Sam read?

$15 - 9 = 6$

How many books did Dixon read?

$6 + 8 = 14$

| 15 |
|----|

| 6 | 9 |
|---|---|

Sam read _____ books.

| 14 |
|----|

| 6 | 8 |
|---|---|

Dixon read _____ books.

**Topic 3** | Lesson 6

Name _____

**Solve & Share**

Carrie has 16 more red apples than green apples. She has 24 green apples. How many red apples are there?

Use any strategy to solve. Use pictures, numbers, or words to explain your thinking and work.

**I can ...**
use pictures, numbers, and words to explain why my thinking and work are correct.

© **Mathematical Practices** MP.3
Also MP.1, MP.5
**Content Standards** 2.NBT.B.9
Also 2.OA.A.1, 2.NBT.B.5

## Thinking Habits
**Construct Arguments**

How can I use math to explain why my work is correct?

Am I using numbers and symbols correctly?

Is my explanation clear?

Is the sum of 48 + 23 the same as the sum of 50 + 21?

Make a math argument.

I can use pictures, words, or numbers to make a math argument and show my work.

I can use an open number line to find each sum.

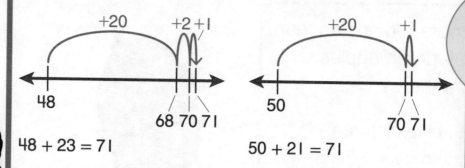

48 + 23 = 71

50 + 21 = 71

Yes, 48 + 23 has the same sum as 50 + 21.

Or I can take 2 from 23 and add it to 48 to make the problems the same. So, the sums must be the same!

48 + 23 = ?

+2   −2

50 + 21 = 71

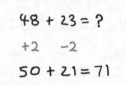

---

**Convince Me!** Are both math arguments above clear and complete? Explain.

☆ **Guided Practice** ☆ Solve. Use pictures, words, or numbers to make a math argument. Show your work.

1. There are 16 chickens in the yard. There are 19 chickens in the barn. There are 30 nesting boxes. Will all of the chickens have a nest? Explain.

_____

_____

_____

_____

## Independent Practice

Solve each problem. Use pictures, words, or numbers to make a math argument. Show your work.

**2.** Greg had 45 sports cards. Jamal gives him 26 more cards. How many sports cards does Greg have now?

AWESOME
MAVERICKS
P. LOVE

_____ sports cards

**3.** Denise drew 8 stars with crayons. Then she drew 6 more stars. Trina drew 5 stars. How many fewer stars did Trina draw than Denise?

_____ fewer stars

# Problem Solving

## Bean Bag Toss

Evan and Pam each throw two bean bags. Points are added for a score. Pam's total score is 100. Which two numbers did Pam's bean bags land on?

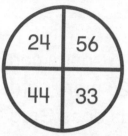

**Bean Bag Toss Game Board**

**4. Make Sense** What information is given? What do you need to find?

_____

_____

_____

**5. Explain** Which numbers did Pam's bags land on? Explain how you know.

_____

_____

_____

_____

**6. Explain** How could you use a hundred chart to solve the problem? Explain.

_____

_____

_____

| 1 | 2 | 3 | 4 | 5 | 6 | 7 | 8 | 9 | 10 |
|---|---|---|---|---|---|---|---|---|---|
| 11 | 12 | 13 | 14 | 15 | 16 | 17 | 18 | 19 | 20 |
| 21 | 22 | 23 | 24 | 25 | 26 | 27 | 28 | 29 | 30 |
| 31 | 32 | 33 | 34 | 35 | 36 | 37 | 38 | 39 | 40 |
| 41 | 42 | 43 | 44 | 45 | 46 | 47 | 48 | 49 | 50 |
| 51 | 52 | 53 | 54 | 55 | 56 | 57 | 58 | 59 | 60 |
| 61 | 62 | 63 | 64 | 65 | 66 | 67 | 68 | 69 | 70 |
| 71 | 72 | 73 | 74 | 75 | 76 | 77 | 78 | 79 | 80 |
| 81 | 82 | 83 | 84 | 85 | 86 | 87 | 88 | 89 | 90 |
| 91 | 92 | 93 | 94 | 95 | 96 | 97 | 98 | 99 | 100 |

Find a partner. Point to a clue. Read the clue.

Look below the clues to find a match. Write the clue letter in the box next to the match.

Find a match for every clue.

**I can ...**
subtract within 20.

© **Content Standard** 2.OA.B.2
**Mathematical Practices** MP.3, MP.6, MP.7, MP.8

**Clues**

**A** Every difference equals 3.

**B** Every difference is less than 2.

**C** Every difference equals 11 − 5.

**D** Exactly two differences are equal.

**E** Every difference is greater than 8.

**F** Exactly three differences are odd.

**G** Every difference equals 16 − 8.

**H** Exactly three differences are even.

| | | | |
|---|---|---|---|
| ☐ 6 − 5<br>8 − 8<br>10 − 10<br>9 − 9 | ☐ 8 − 6<br>12 − 8<br>15 − 8<br>4 − 0 | ☐ 18 − 9<br>16 − 7<br>11 − 2<br>10 − 1 | ☐ 10 − 8<br>9 − 4<br>6 − 2<br>14 − 9 |
| ☐ 17 − 9<br>9 − 1<br>13 − 5<br>12 − 4 | ☐ 14 − 8<br>12 − 6<br>8 − 2<br>13 − 7 | ☐ 11 − 6<br>5 − 3<br>14 − 7<br>12 − 3 | ☐ 12 − 9<br>9 − 6<br>11 − 8<br>10 − 7 |

A-Z
Glossary

**Word List**
- bar diagram
- break apart
- compensation
- mental math
- ones
- open number line
- tens

## Understand Vocabulary

**1.** Circle the numbers that have a 3 in the ones place.

     33     45     13     38

**2.** Cross out the numbers that do **NOT** have an 8 in the tens place.

     80     18     78     89

**3.** Write an equation to show how to break apart 54 by place value.

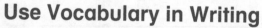

**4.** Use the open number line to find 38 + 23. Add the tens and then add the ones.

## Use Vocabulary in Writing

**5.** Describe a way to find 47 + 18. Use terms from the Word List.

Name _____

**Set A**

You can use a hundred chart to help
you add. Find 62 + 12.

Start at 62.
Move down
1 row to add
the 1 ten in
12.

| 51 | 52 | 53 | 54 | 55 | 56 | 57 | 58 | 59 | 60 |
| 61 | 62 | 63 | 64 | 65 | 66 | 67 | 68 | 69 | 70 |
| 71 | 72 | 73 | 74 | 75 | 76 | 77 | 78 | 79 | 80 |
| 81 | 82 | 83 | 84 | 85 | 86 | 87 | 88 | 89 | 90 |
| 91 | 92 | 93 | 94 | 95 | 96 | 97 | 98 | 99 | 100 |

Then move over
2 columns to add
the 2 ones in 12. So, 62 + 12 = _74_ .

Use a hundred chart to
find each sum.

1. 85 + 15 = _____

2. 60 + 23 = _____

**Set B**

You can use an open number line to
find 49 + 32.

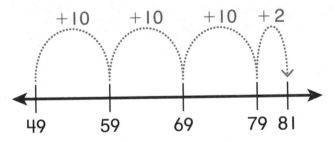

Place 49 on the number line. There are 3 tens
in 32. So, count on by 10 three times. There
are 2 ones in 32. So, count on 2 from 79.

So, 49 + 32 = _81_ .

Use an open number line to
find each sum.

3. 35 + 13 = _____

4. 47 + 26 = _____

Find $55 + 17$.
Break apart $17$ into $10 + 7$.

$$55 \quad + \quad 17 = ?$$

| 55 | | 10 | 7 |

Add tens: $55 + 10 = 65$

Add ones: $65 + 7 = 72$

So, $55 + 17 = \underline{72}$.

Break apart the second
addend to find the sum.
Show your work.

**5.** $53 + 28 = \underline{\hspace{1cm}}$

**6.** $78 + 19 = \underline{\hspace{1cm}}$

Find $48 + 27$.

$48$ is close to $50$. So, take $2$ from $27$
and give it to $48$ to make $50$.

$48 + 27 = ?$

$+2 \quad -2$

$50 + 25 = ?$

| 20 | 5 |

$\underline{50} + \underline{20} + \underline{5} = \underline{75}$

So, $48 + 27 = \underline{75}$.

Use compensation to make numbers
that are easier to add. Then solve.
Show your work.

**7.** $17 + 46 = \underline{\hspace{1cm}}$

**8.** $29 + 57 = \underline{\hspace{1cm}}$

TOPIC
3

## Set E

You can use different strategies and tools to find a sum.

You can:
- Use a hundred chart
- Use an open number line
- Break apart one addend
- Use compensation

Solve. Show your work.

9. Ted's puzzle has 37 more pieces than his brother's puzzle. His brother's puzzle has 48 pieces. How many pieces does Ted's puzzle have?

_____ pieces

## Set F

Marla walks 12 blocks on Monday.
On Tuesday, she walks 4 fewer blocks.
How many blocks does Marla walk in all?

Blocks Marla walks on Tuesday:

$\underline{12} - \underline{4} = \underline{8}$

Blocks Marla walks on Monday and Tuesday:

$\underline{12} + \underline{8} = \underline{20}$

$\underline{20}$ blocks

Solve the two-step problem.

10. Wyatt has 16 crayons.
He buys 24 new crayons.
Then he finds 7 more crayons.
How many crayons does Wyatt have now?

_____ ⊕ _____ = _____

_____ ⊕ _____ = _____

_____ crayons

## Thinking Habits

**Construct Arguments**

How can I use math to explain my work?

Am I using numbers and symbols correctly?

Is my explanation clear?

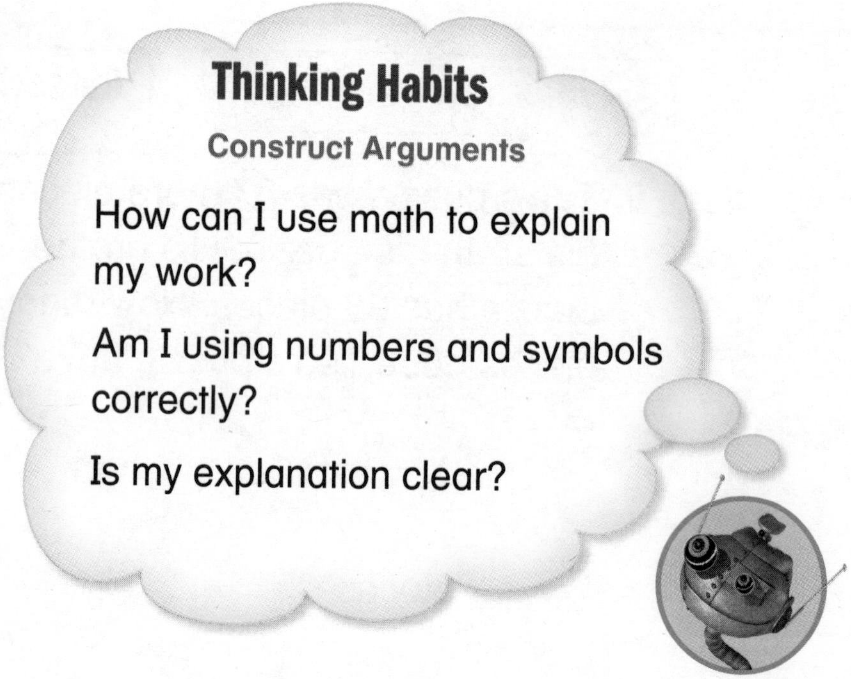

Solve the problem. Use words and numbers to make a math argument.

11. A second-grade class sets a goal to collect 70 cans. One week they collect 38 cans. The next week they collect 35 cans. Do they meet their goal?

_____

_____

_____

_____

_____

_____

Name _____

**1.** Which have a sum of 43? Choose all that apply.

☐ 33 + 10

☐ 28 + 13

☐ 10 + 33

☐ 19 + 24

☐ 10 + 21

**2.** Terry has 63 crayons.
She gets 25 more crayons.
How many crayons does Terry have in all? Show your work.

_____ crayons

**3.** Which equation does this number line show?

Ⓐ 57 + 28 = 85    Ⓒ 57 + 33 = 90

Ⓑ 57 + 38 = 95    Ⓓ 57 + 39 = 96

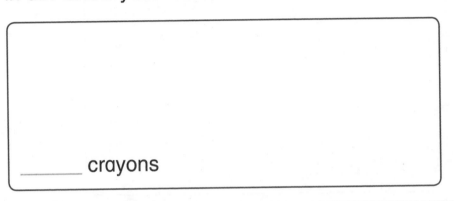

**4.** Use the numbers on the cards. Write the missing numbers under the number line to show how to find the sum of 40 + 35.

 75    60    50   70

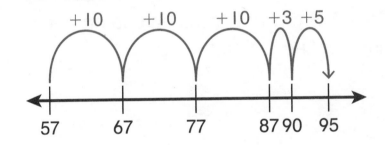

**5.** Colin has 54 pennies and 28 nickels. How many coins does Colin have?

Break apart the second addend to solve. Show your work.

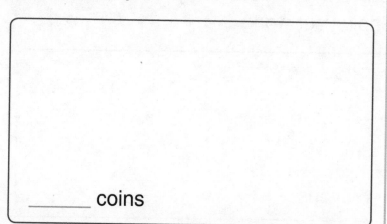

_____ coins

**6.** Show how to add 68 + 16 using the open number line.

$68 + 16 =$ _____

**7. Part A** Show how you can use an open number line to find 44 + 27.

$44 + 27 =$ _____

**Part B** In words, tell how you used the open number line to find the sum.

**8.** Which have a sum of 70? Choose all that apply.

☐ 35 + 35        ☐ 40 + 30        ☐ 45 + 45        ☐ 50 + 20        ☐ 30 + 30

**Topic 3** | Assessment Practice

Name _____

## Popcorn Sales

A second-grade class is selling popcorn to help pay for a field trip.

This table shows how many boxes some students have sold.

| Number of Popcorn Boxes Sold | |
|---|---|
| Ted | 21 |
| Nancy | 19 |
| Darnell | 28 |
| Mary | 34 |
| Elena | 43 |

Performance
Task

1. How many boxes of popcorn did Ted and Mary sell in all? Use the open number line to solve. Show your work.

⟵——————————————⟶

_____ boxes

2. James says that Mary and Nancy sold more boxes in all than Darnell and Ted sold in all. Do you agree with him?

Circle:        **Yes**                **No**

Explain your answer.

_____

_____

_____

_____

**3.** Which two students sold a total of 55 boxes? Use any strategy to solve. Show your work.

Circle the names of the two students.

Ted            Nancy            Darnell

Mary            Elena

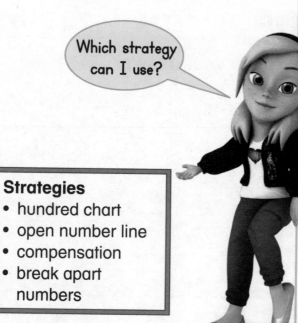

Which strategy can I use?

**Strategies**
• hundred chart
• open number line
• compensation
• break apart numbers

**4.** Nancy sold 18 fewer boxes than Lucas. How many boxes did Lucas sell?

**Part A** Solve the problem. Show your work and explain your thinking.

_____ boxes

**Part B** Look at the list of strategies at the left. To show that your answer in Part A is correct, use a different strategy to solve the problem.

**Topic 3** | Performance Task

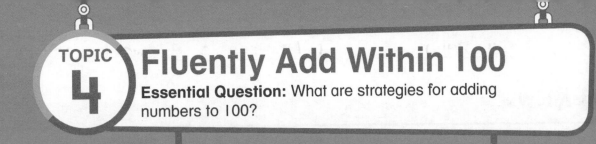

# TOPIC 4 Fluently Add Within 100

**Essential Question:** What are strategies for adding numbers to 100?

**Digital Resources**

Interactive Student Edition · Activity · Visual Learning · Video · Practice

Assessment · Games · Tools · Glossary

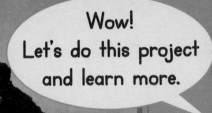

The islands of Hawaii began as volcanoes!

You can still see some volcanoes if you visit Hawaii.

Wow! Let's do this project and learn more.

## enVision STEM Project: Making and Using Models

**Find Out** Find and share books about Hawaii and volcanoes. Make a model of a volcano that becomes an island. Tell about how the island can change over a long time.

**Journal: Make a Book** Show what you learn in a book. In your book, also:

- Draw pictures to show how volcanoes can become islands.

- Show how you can use models to help you add numbers to 100.

Name _____

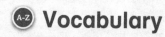 **Review What You Know**

**A-Z** **Vocabulary**

**1.** Circle the **tens** digit in each number.

73

53

82

**2.** Circle the **ones** digit in each number.

34

43

97

**3.** **Break apart** 23 into tens and ones.

23 = _____ tens and

_____ ones

**Mental Math**

**4.** Use mental math to find each sum.

34 + 10 = _____

50 + 5 = _____

20 + 40 = _____

**Open Number Line**

**5.** Use the open number line to find 39 + 15.

39 + 15 = _____

**Math Story**

**6.** Stacy has 17 marbles. Diana gives her 22 marbles. How many marbles does Stacy have now?

_____ marbles

Name _____

**PROJECT 4A**

**Where can you bike near home?**

**Project:** Make a Bike Trail Brochure

**PROJECT 4B**

**What kinds of coral grow in Florida?**

**Project:** Build a Coral Model

## What do you collect?

**Project:** Display a Rock and
Leaf Collection

## How much does it cost to visit the Kennedy Space Center?

**Project:** Make a Space
Center Poster

Name _____

**Solve & Share**

Leslie collects 36 rocks. Her brother collects 27 rocks. How many rocks do they collect in all?

Use place-value blocks to help you solve. Show your place-value blocks.

**I can ...**
use models to add 2-digit numbers and then explain my work.

© **Content Standards** 2.NBT.B.5
Also 2.NBT.B.9
**Mathematical Practices** MP.3, MP.4, MP.5

You can make 36 and 27 with place-value blocks.

_____ rocks

Find 47 + 26.

You can show 47 and 26 with place-value blocks.

**4 tens**    **7 ones**      **2 tens**   **6 ones**

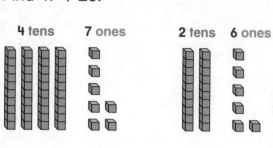

Join the tens and ones. **Regroup** if needed.

**6 tens**      **13 ones**

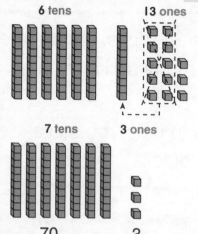

Regroup 13 ones as 1 ten and 3 ones.

**7 tens**    **3 ones**

70          3       So, 47 + 26 = __73__.

---

**Convince Me!** When do you need to regroup when adding?

**Guided Practice**   Add. Use place-value blocks to find each sum. Regroup if needed.

**1.** 32 + 29 = _____

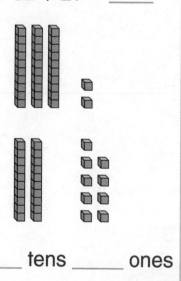

_____ tens _____ ones

**2.** 24 + 52 = _____

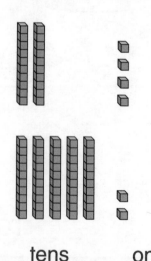

_____ tens _____ ones

**3.** 15 + 38 = _____

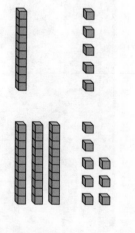

_____ tens _____ one

Name _____

**Solve & Share**

Wendy picked 35 pears. Toni picked 49 pears. How many pears did they pick in all?

Use place-value blocks to help explain your work.

**I can …**
add numbers using place value and properties of operations.

**Content Standards** 2.NBT.B.5 Also 2.OA.A.1, 2.NBT.B.9
**Mathematical Practices** MP.1, MP.3, MP.4

_____ pears

Find 36 + 59.

**One Way**
Use quick drawings for the addends.

3 tens 6 ones     5 tens 9 ones

Draw blocks. Use a line for each ten and a dot for each one.

Join the tens and ones.
Regroup if needed.

8 tens          15 ones

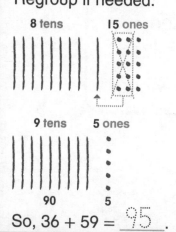

9 tens     5 ones

90          5

So, 36 + 59 = __95__.

**Another Way**

```
  3 tens 6 ones
+ 5 tens 9 ones
───────────────
  8 tens 15 ones
```

Think: 15 ones is 1 ten 5 ones.

8 tens 1 ten 5 ones
$80 + 10 + 5 = 95$

Does your answer make sense?

**Convince Me!** Ken adds 43 + 27. His sum is 60. Is he correct? Explain.

☆**Guided Practice**☆ Add. Use place value. Draw blocks or use another way.

**1.** 12 + 23 = ____

**2.** 18 + 42 = ____

```
  1 ten  8 ones
+ 4 tens 2 ones
───────────────
  5 tens 10 ones
```

10 ones = 1 ten

5 tens + 1 ten = 6 tens

**3.** 33 + 48 = ____

**Solve & Share**

Ms. Kim's class has 25 students.
Mr. Will's class has 36 students.
Both classes go on a field trip. How many students are on the trip?

Draw place-value blocks to help you solve the problem.

**I can ...**
add using place value and partial sums.

© **Content Standards** 2.NBT.B.5
Also 2.OA.A.1, 2.NBT.B.9
**Mathematical Practices** MP.4, MP.7

_____ students

Visual Learning
A-Z Glossary

Find 57 + 28.

| Tens | Ones |
|------|------|
| 5 | 7 |
| + 2 | 8 |

I can use place-value blocks to add and record partial sums.

**Add the tens.**

5 tens + 2 tens = 7 tens

**Add the ones.**

7 ones + 8 ones = 15 ones

70 and 15 are the partial sums.

**Write the partial sums.**

| Tens | Ones |
|------|------|
| 5 | 7 |
| + 2 | 8 |
| 50 + 20 = | 7 | 0 |
| 7 + 8 = | 1 | 5 |

**Then add the partial sums to find the sum.**

| Tens | Ones |
|------|------|
| 5 | 7 |
| + 2 | 8 |
| 50 + 20 = | 7 | 0 |
| 7 + 8 = | 1 | 5 |
| Sum = | 8 | 5 |

So, 57 + 28 = 85.

**Convince Me!** Can you add the ones first and then the tens when finding 57 + 28 using partial sums? Explain.

**Guided Practice** Add. Use partial sums. Draw blocks if you need to.

1. 24 + 13

| Tens | Ones |
|------|------|
| 2 | 4 |
| + 1 | 3 |
| 20 + 10 = | 3 | 0 |
| 4 + 3 = | | 7 |
| Sum = | | |

2. 68 + 7

| Tens | Ones |
|------|------|
| 6 | 8 |
| + | 7 |
| 60 + 0 = | | |
| 8 + 7 = | | |
| Sum = | | |

146 one hundred forty-six

Topic 4 | Lesson 3

**Name** _____

## Solve & Share

Add 46 + 26.

Explain how you solved the problem.

**I can ...**
add numbers using place value and partial sums.

© **Content Standards** 2.NBT.B.5 Also 2.NBT.B.9
**Mathematical Practices** MP.1, MP.2, MP.3

_____

_____

_____

Find 56 + 17.

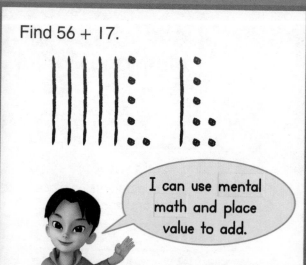

I can use mental math and place value to add.

Mentally break apart the numbers using tens and ones.

56 + 17 = ?

| 50 | | 10 |
| 6 | | 7 |

Find the partial sums.
Find the sum.

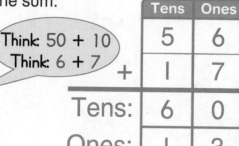

Think: 50 + 10
Think: 6 + 7

| | Tens | Ones |
|---|---|---|
| | 5 | 6 |
| + | 1 | 7 |
| Tens: | 6 | 0 |
| Ones: | 1 | 3 |
| Sum: | 7 | 3 |

So, 56 + 17 = 73.

---

**Convince Me!** Roger found 54 + 27. His sum was 71. Is he correct? Why or why not? Use partial sums to check.

☆ **Guided Practice** ☆   Write the addition problem. Use partial sums. Add any way you choose. Show your work.

**1.** 34 + 17

| | Tens | Ones |
|---|---|---|
| | | |
| + | | |
| Tens: | | |
| Ones: | | |
| Sum: | | |

**2.** 52 + 31

| | Tens | Ones |
|---|---|---|
| | | |
| + | | |
| Tens: | | |
| Ones: | | |
| Sum: | | |

**3.** 35 + 26

| | Tens | Ones |
|---|---|---|
| | | |
| + | | |
| Tens: | | |
| Ones: | | |
| Sum: | | |

**Lesson 4-5**

**Break Apart Numbers and Add Using Mental Math**

**Solve & Share**

Monica has 24 crayons. Paul has 64 crayons. How many crayons do they have in all?

Use place-value blocks or draw a picture to explain your work.

**I can ...**
add within 100 using place-value strategies.

© **Content Standards** 2.NBT.B.5 Also 2.NBT.B.9
**Mathematical Practices** MP.2, MP.7, MP.8

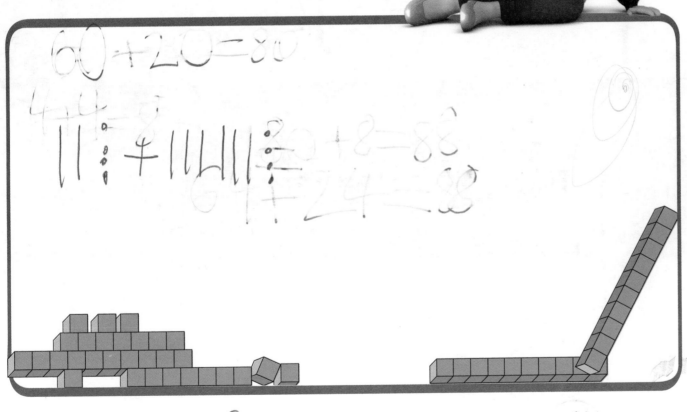

60 + 20 = 80

40 = 8

||| + ||||||  80 + 2 = 88

64 + 24 = 88

88 crayons

Find 27 + 35.

*You can break apart numbers in different ways to add mentally.*

**One Way**

Break apart the second addend to make a 10.

27 + 35 = ?

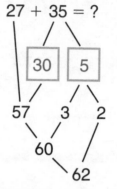

3    32

30

62

So, 27 + 35 = 62.

**Another Way**

Break apart the second addend into tens and ones.

27 + 35 = ?

30    5

57    3    2

60

62

*Add 30 + 27 = 57. Next, 57 + 3 = 60. Then, 60 + 2 = 62.*

So, 27 + 35 = 62.

**Convince Me!** Explain one way you can break apart numbers to find 14 + 32.

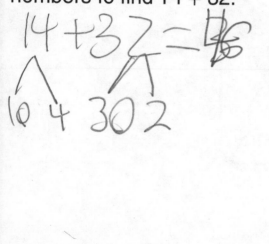

$14 + 32 = 46$

10  4  30  2

☆ **Guided Practice** ☆  Find each sum using mental math. Draw pictures of blocks if needed.

1.  17 + 52 = __69__

50    2

67

69

2.  __92__ = 69 + 23

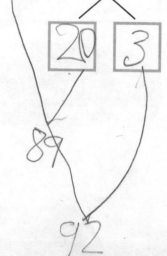

20    3

89

92

Name _____

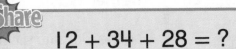
$12 + 34 + 28 = ?$

Tom says he can find the sum by adding 28 and 12 first. He says he can add 34 to that sum to find the total.

Do you agree? Use pictures, words, and numbers to make a math argument.

Then solve the problem. Show your work.

**I can ...**
add three or four 2-digit numbers.

**Content Standards** 2.NBT.B.6
Also 2 NBT.B.5, 2.NBT.B.9
**Mathematical Practices** MP.2, MP.3, MP.8

$12 + 34 + 28 =$ _____

 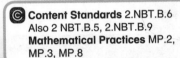

Find $24 + 35 + 16 + 17$.

Show each addend by drawing tens and ones. Join the tens. Join the ones. Then add the partial sums.

**One Way**

7 tens and 22 ones

$70 + 20 + 2 = 92$

Write the partial sums and find the sum.

| Tens | Ones |
|------|------|
| 2 | 4 |
| 3 | 5 |
| 1 | 6 |
| + 1 | 7 |
| Tens: 7 | 0 |
| Ones: 2 | 2 |
| Sum: 9 | 2 |

**Another Way**

Use the Commutative Property.

$24 + 16 + 35 + 17 = ?$

**40**          **52**

$40 + 52 = 92$

So, $24 + 35 + 16 + 17 = 92$.

**Convince Me!** Look above. Why do you think the order of the addends changed? Why do you think 24 and 16 were added together?

☆ **Guided Practice** Add. Use any strategy. Show your work.

1. $18 + 15 + 12 = $ ____

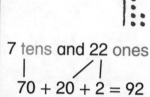

$18 + 12 + 15 = ?$

$30 \quad + 15 = ?$

$30 + 15 = 45$

2. $11 + 14 + 39 = $ ____

3. $21 + 14 + 41 + 22 = $ ____

4. $21 + 15 + 32 + 25 = $ ____

**Topic 4 | Lesson 6**

## Independent Practice ☆ Add. Use any strategy. Show your work.

**5.** $27 + 21 + 13 =$ _____

**6.** $16 + 32 + 28 =$ _____

**7.** $32 + 14 + 42 =$ _____

**8.** $25 + 17 + 24 + 15 =$ _____

**9.** $32 + 16 + 18 + 31 =$ _____

**10.** $37 + 11 + 13 + 38 =$ _____

## Algebra Find the missing numbers.

**11.** $8 + 3 + \boxed{\phantom{0}} + 2 = 18$

**12.** $5 + \boxed{\phantom{0}} + 6 + 5 = 19$

**13.** $7 + 27 + 23 + \boxed{\phantom{0}} = 61$

**14.** $\boxed{\phantom{0}} + 24 + 18 + 4 = 52$

**15.** 28 trucks are blue.
32 trucks are yellow.
17 trucks are green.
11 trucks are pink.
How many trucks are there in all?

_____ trucks

**16.** Joel won 19 tickets in March, 24 tickets in April, 23 tickets in May, and 16 tickets in June. How many tickets does Joel have in all?

_____ tickets

**17. Higher Order Thinking** Henry is adding the numbers 24, 18, and 36. He makes a ten to add. Which ones digits does Henry add first? Explain.

_____

_____

_____

**18.** ☑ **Assessment Practice** Find the sum. Use any strategy. Show your work.

$$25 + 16 + 15 + 38 = \underline{\quad}$$

Name _____

Solve & Share

Maria has 39 stickers. Sally has 28 stickers. They found 14 more stickers. How many stickers do they have in all?

Solve. Use any strategy. Explain how you found the answer.

**I can ...**
use mental math, strategies, and models to add two, three, or four numbers.

Content Standards 2.NBT.B.6 Also 2 NBT.B.5, 2.NBT.B.9
Mathematical Practices MP.4, MP.7

$$39 + 28 + 14 = 81$$

30    9    20    8    10    4

60    21

81

81 _____ stickers

Find 27 + 38 + 12 + 3.
**One Way:** Use partial sums.

| Tens | Ones |
|------|------|
| 2 | (7) |
| 3 | 8 |
| 1 | 2 |
| + | (3) |
| Tens: 6 | 0 |
| Ones: 2 | 0 |
| Sum: 8 | 0 |

Look for compatible numbers to make tens.
7 + 3 = 10
8 + 2 = 10
10 + 10 = 20

**Another Way:** Break apart the addends by place value. Then use mental math.

Add the tens.
**20 + 30 + 10 = 60**

Add the ones.
**7 + 8 + 2 + 3 = 20**

Add the partial sums.
**60 + 20 = 80**

**Another Way**

You can also add the numbers in a different order.

**30**

27 + 38 + 12 + 3 = ?

**50**

30 + 50 = 80
So, 27 + 38 + 12 + 3 = 80.

---

**Convince Me!** Find the sum of
14 + 28 + 33 + 22. Explain.

☆ **Guided Practice**   Add. Use any strategy. Show your work.

1. 18 + 43 + 12 = 73
10 + 40 + 10 = 60
8 + 3 + 2 = 13
60 + 13 = 73

2. 29 + 47 = 76
20 + 40 = 60
9 + 7 16

3. 9 + 34 + 21 = 64
1
10 + 34 + 20 = 64

4. 33 + 27 + 18 + 13 = 91

## Solve & Share

The second graders take a trip to a nature center. The Green Class sees 23 animals. The Blue Class sees 14 animals. The Yellow Class sees 32 animals. How many animals do they see in all?

Solve using drawings, models, or an equation. Be prepared to explain your work.

**I can ...**

use drawings, models, and equations to solve one- and two-step problems.

© **Content Standards** 2.OA.A.1 Also 2.NBT.B.5, 2.NBT.B.6 **Mathematical Practices** MP.1, MP.4, MP.8

_____ animals

Visual Learning    A-Z Glossary

Aimee and Devin count 36 butterflies. Suddenly, more butterflies join them. Now, there are 53 butterflies.

How many new butterflies join them?

53

| 36 | ? |

$36 + ? = 53$

The total is 53. The first group has 36 butterflies. I will use a bar diagram to model the problem.

I can use mental math to find $36 + ? = 53$.

Think:   $36 + 10 = 46$
$46 + 4 = 50$
$50 + 3 = 53$

$10 + 4 + 3 = 17$

So, $36 + \underline{17} = 53$.

So, 17 butterflies join them.

Check your work.

$$\begin{array}{r} 36 \\ + 17 \\ \hline \end{array}$$
Tens: 40
Ones: 13
Sum: 53

The answer makes sense.

$36 + 17 = 53$

---

**Convince Me!** What is a different way you can use mental math to find $36 + ? = 53$?

**☆Guided Practice☆** Use the bar diagram and mental math to solve each problem. Then check your work.

1. Bruce buys 18 eggs. He uses 10 of them for baking. Then he buys 36 more eggs. How many eggs does Bruce have now?

18

| 10 | 8 |

☐

| 8 | 36 |

Check:

$\underline{18} \ominus \underline{10} = \underline{8}$

$\underline{8} \oplus \underline{36} = \underline{\phantom{00}}$

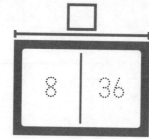

_____ eggs

**Independent Practice**   Use the bar diagram(s) and mental math to solve each problem. Then check your work.

**2.** Ella has 34 more buttons than Julio. Julio has 49 buttons. How many buttons does Ella have?

Check:

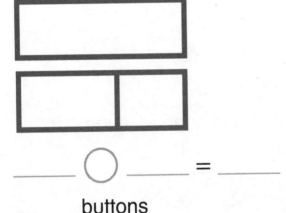

_____ ◯ _____ = _____

_____ buttons

**3.** 20 students are on the bus. Then 10 students get off the bus. Next, 15 students get on the bus. How many students are on the bus now?

Check:

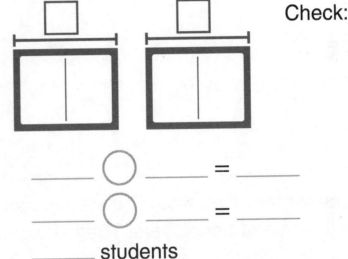

_____ ◯ _____ = _____

_____ ◯ _____ = _____

_____ students

**4.** Wendy has 14 more crayons than Oscar. Oscar has 54 crayons. How many crayons does Wendy have?

Check:

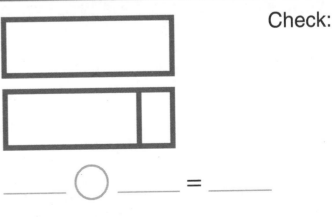

The bar diagram helps you see how the numbers are related.

_____ ◯ _____ = _____

_____ crayons

**Topic 4** | Lesson 8

one hundred sixty-seven  **167**

## Problem Solving ☆ Solve each problem. Show your work.

5. **Make Sense** Mariah has 17 figs. Kendra has 20 more figs than Mariah. Toby has 33 more figs than Kendra. How many figs do Kendra and Toby each have?

**Step 1:**
How many figs does Kendra have?

_____ ◯ _____ = _____ _____ figs

**Step 2:**
How many figs does Toby have?

_____ ◯ _____ = _____ _____ figs

> Solve one step at a time.

6. **Higher Order Thinking** 8 girls and some boys are in the pool. In all, 17 children are in the pool. Then some more boys jump in the pool. Now there are 13 boys in the pool. How many more boys jumped in the pool?

**Step 1:**

_____ ◯ _____ = _____

**Step 2:**

_____ ◯ _____ = _____

_____ more boys jumped in the pool

7. ☑ **Assessment Practice** The soccer coach has 18 shirts. She gives 9 of the shirts to some of her players. Then she gets 11 more shirts. How many shirts does the coach have left?

Show how you can solve the problem in two steps.

**Step 1:**                    **Step 2:**

The coach has _____ shirts left.

Name _____

Kim puts 25 toys into an empty toy box.
Then she puts 17 more toys in the toy box.
How many toys are in the box in all?

Use a model to show the problem. Be ready to explain
how your model helps you solve the problem.

**I can ...**
make models to help solve
math problems.

Ⓒ **Mathematical Practices** MP.4 Also
MP.1, MP.3
**Content Standards** 2.OA.A.1 Also
2.NBT.B.5, 2.NBT.B.6, 2.NBT.B.9

**Thinking Habits**

Can I write an
equation or use a
drawing, diagram,
table, graph, or
objects to show
the problem?

_____ toys

Eric has 29 crayons. He buys a box of 16 crayons. How many crayons does Eric have in all?

Here are some models you can use or make.

**Models**
arrays
bar diagrams
drawings
equations

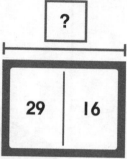

Which model can I use to show this problem?

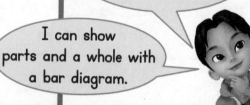

?

29 | 16

$29 + 16 = ?$

I can also model the problem with an equation. An equation uses numbers and symbols.

I can show parts and a whole with a bar diagram.

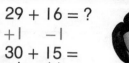
$29 + 16 = ?$
$+1 \quad -1$
$30 + 15 =$
$30 + 10 + 5 = 45$

So, $29 + 16 = 45$.

I can use any strategy to find the sum.

So, Eric has 45 crayons in all.

---

**Convince Me!** How does drawing a bar diagram or writing an equation model a problem? Is there another way to model the problem?

**Guided Practice** Complete the bar diagram. Write an equation to model the problem. Then solve.

1. Flora has 24 books about birds. She has 18 books about bugs. How many books is that?

   $\underline{24}$ $\oplus$ $\underline{18}$ = $\underline{\ ?\ }$ books

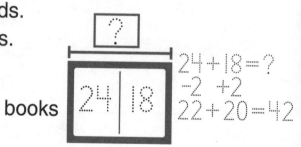

?

24 | 18

$24 + 18 = ?$
$-2 \quad +2$
$22 + 20 = 42$

2. Barb saw 14 cars on Smith Street. She saw 8 cars on Alfred Street. How many more cars did Barb see on Smith Street?

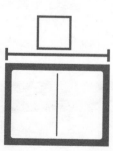

   _____ ◯ _____ = _____ cars

**Topic 4 | Lesson 9**

Tools  Assessment

Make a model to show each problem. Then use the model to solve. Show your work.

**3.** Avi takes 16 pictures.
Then he takes 17 more pictures.
How many pictures does Avi take?

Remember, you can use different models. Be ready to explain how your model shows the problem!

**4.** Tina picks 55 blueberries. Next, Tina eats 6 of these blueberries. Then she picks 27 more. How many blueberries does she have now?

**5.** Raj finds 47 acorns in his front yard. He finds 29 acorns in his back yard. How many acorns does Raj find in all?

# Problem Solving

### African Safari

The Santos family is on an African safari.
The chart at the right shows the number
of animals they see.

How many animals do they see?

| Number of Animals | |
|---|---|
| Giraffes | 15 |
| Elephants | 9 |
| Lions | 16 |
| Zebras | 11 |

6. **Make Sense** What do you know? What
are you asked to find?

_____

_____

_____

7. **Model** Make a model to help you find the
number of animals they see. Be ready to
explain why you chose the model you did.

8. **Model** What other model could you use to show the
problem? Make another model. Explain which model you
think is better.

_____

_____

Name _____

**Point & Tally**

Find a partner. Get paper and a pencil.
Each partner chooses a different color: light blue or dark blue.

Partner 1 and Partner 2 each point to a black number at the same time. Both partners add those numbers.

If the answer is on your color, you get a tally mark.
Work until one partner gets twelve tally marks.

**I can ...**
add within 20.

© **Content Standard** 2.OA.B.2
**Mathematical Practices** MP.3,
MP.6, MP.7, MP.8

**Partner 1**

| 7 |
| 4 |
| 9 |
| 6 |
| 8 |
| 5 |

| 13 | 17 | 14 | 10 | 9 | 12 |
| 15 | 11 | 8 | 18 | 13 | 16 |

**Partner 2**

| 8 |
| 6 |
| 5 |
| 4 |
| 7 |
| 9 |

**Tally Marks for Partner 1**

**Tally Marks for Partner 2**

A-Z
Glossary

**Word List**
- addends
- compatible numbers
- ones
- partial sum
- regroup
- sum
- tens

## Understand Vocabulary

Use the problem at the right.
Write *partial sum* or *sum* for each.

| Tens | Ones |
|------|------|
| 6 | 8 |
| + 1 | 9 |
| 7 | 0 |
| 1 | 7 |
| 8 | 7 |

1. 70 is a _____.

2. 17 is a _____.

3. 87 is the _____.

4. Use the ones column in the problem at the right. Which compatible numbers can you add to make a ten two different ways?

Write two different equations.

| Tens | Ones |
|------|------|
| 3 | 8 |
| 1 | 4 |
| 2 | 2 |
| + | 6 |

## Use Vocabulary in Writing

5. Solve 27 + 35 by breaking apart both addends. Tell how you solved the problem. Use terms from the Word List.

TOPIC 4

**Set A**

Find 55 + 17. Use place-value blocks. Show the addends. Join the tens and ones. Regroup if needed.

**Reteaching**

Add. Use place-value blocks to show your work. Regroup if needed.

1. 36 + 23 = _____

2. 19 + 44 = _____

10 ones = I ten

Count blocks.

7 tens  2 ones

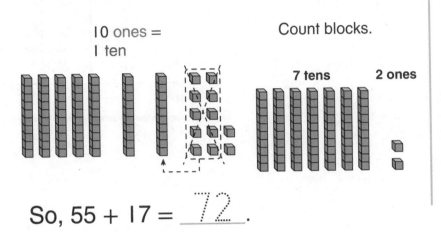

So, 55 + 17 = _72_.

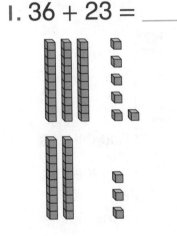

_____ tens _____ ones

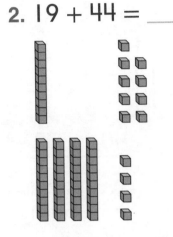

_____ tens _____ ones

**Set B**

Find 24 + 49. Draw place-value blocks to show the addends. Join the tens and ones. Regroup if needed.

Add. Use place value and draw blocks.

3. 64 + 13 = _____

4. 27 + 56 = _____

10 ones = I ten

Count blocks.

7 tens  3 ones

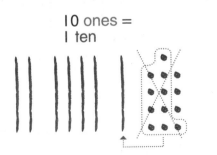

70  3

So, 24 + 49 = _73_.

You can draw blocks and use partial sums to find 46 + 37.

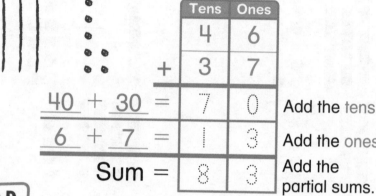

| | Tens | Ones |
|---|---|---|
| | 4 | 6 |
| + | 3 | 7 |
| 40 + 30 = | 7 | 0 |
| 6 + 7 = | 1 | 3 |
| Sum = | 8 | 3 |

Add the tens.
Add the ones.
Add the partial sums.

Add. Draw place-value blocks and use partial sums.

5. 33 + 57
**Drawings:**

| | Tens | Ones |
|---|---|---|
| | 3 | 3 |
| + | 5 | 7 |
| ___ + ___ = | | |
| ___ + ___ = | | |
| Sum = | | |

Find 29 + 63. You can break apart the addends and use partial sums.

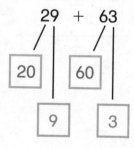

| | Tens | Ones |
|---|---|---|
| | 2 | 9 |
| + | 6 | 3 |
| Tens: | 8 | 0 |
| Ones: | 1 | 2 |
| Sum: | 9 | 2 |

Add. Break apart the addends and use partial sums.

6.

| | Tens | Ones |
|---|---|---|
| | 1 | 7 |
| + | 7 | 7 |
| Tens: | | |
| Ones: | | |
| Sum: | | |

7.

| | Tens | Ones |
|---|---|---|
| | 2 | 4 |
| + | 3 | 8 |
| Tens: | | |
| Ones: | | |
| Sum: | | |

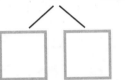

**Set E**

Find 32 + 19. Break apart the second addend and add mentally.

32 + 19 = ____ ?

[number bond diagram: 19 breaks into 10 and 9; 9 breaks into 8 and 1; 42, 8, 1; 50; 51]

Add __32__ + __10__ = __42__

Next __42__ + __8__ = __50__

Then __50__ + __1__ = __51__

Break apart the second addend to add. Show your work.

8. 24 + 55 = ____

[blank boxes]

9. 64 + 27 = ____

[blank boxes]

**Set F**

Use partial sums to find 65 + 7 + 13.

| Tens | Ones |
|------|------|
| 6 | 5 |
|   | 7 |
| + 1 | 3 |
| Tens: 7 | 0 |
| Ones: 1 | 5 |
| Sum: 8 | 5 |

← Look for
← compatible
numbers
to make tens.

7 + 3 = 10

So, 65 + 7 + 13 = __85__

Add using partial sums.

10.

| Tens | Ones |
|------|------|
| 2 | 2 |
| 2 | 1 |
|   | 9 |
| + 1 | 8 |
| Tens: | |
| Ones: | |
| Sum: | |

11.

| Tens | Ones |
|------|------|
| 4 | 1 |
| 1 | 5 |
| 2 | 9 |
| + 1 | 0 |
| Tens: | |
| Ones: | |
| Sum: | |

27 students are eating lunch.
More students join them.
Now 63 students are eating lunch.
How many students joined them?

Write an equation: 27 + ? = 63
Count on to find the missing addend:

$27 + 30 = 57$   |   $30 + 3 + 3 = \underline{36}$
$57 + 3 = 60$   |   $27 + \underline{36} = 63$
$60 + 3 = 63$   |

So, 36 students joined them.

Complete the bar diagram, write an equation, and solve.

12. Lana has 24 crayons.
Then she gets some
more crayons.
Now she has 42 crayons.
How many crayons does
Lana get?

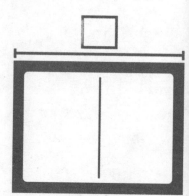

### Thinking Habits

**Model with Math**

Can I use a drawing,
diagram, table, graph, or
objects to show the problem?

Can I write an equation to
show the problem?

Make a model and solve the problem.

13. Students ride buses to the museum.
28 students ride in Bus A.
27 students ride in Bus B.
How many students ride in both buses?

Name _____

## Our Pets

Students draw pictures of their pets.
The chart shows the number of pets the
students have.

| Number of Pets | |
|---|---|
| Dogs 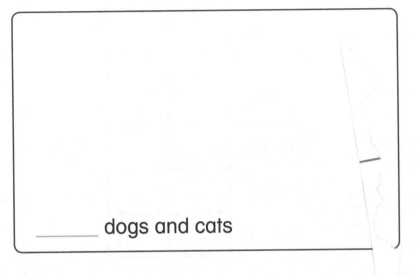 | 41 |
| Cats | 29 |
| Rabbits | 6 |
| Fish | 24 |

Performance Task

1. How many dogs and cats do
the students have?
Show your work.

_____ dogs and cats

2. How many cats and fish do
the students have?
Show your work.

_____ cats and fish

**3.** Use partial sums to find how many cats, rabbits, and fish the students have. Be sure to check your work.

| | Tens | Ones |
|---|---|---|
| | | |
| | | |
| **+** | | |
| Tens: | | |
| Ones: | | |
| Sum: | | |

How many cats, rabbits, and fish in all?

_____ cats, rabbits, and fish

**4.** Explain how to use partial sums to add.

_____

_____

_____

**5.** The students also draw pictures of 10 hamsters, 19 birds, and 5 mice.

### Part A

Complete the model to show how to find the total number of hamsters, birds and mice.

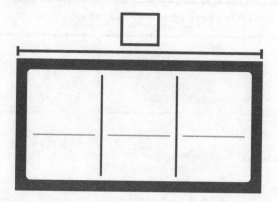

### Part B

Complete the equation to show how many hamsters, birds, and mice they draw. Then write the total.

_____ hamsters, birds, and mice

**Topic 4** | Performance Task

# Subtract Within 100 Using Strategies

**Essential Question:** What are strategies for subtracting numbers to 100?

**Digital Resources**

Interactive Student Edition   Activity   Visual Learning   Video   Practice

Assessment   Games   Tools   Glossary

Look at the big pieces of ice in the water!

How can heating and cooling change water and ice?

Wow! Let's do this project and learn more.

## enVision® STEM Project: Heating, Cooling, and Subtraction

**Find Out** Have an adult help you heat and cool water and other materials. Find out if water and ice can change back and forth. Find out if heating and cooling an egg can change it back and forth.

**Journal: Make a Book** Show what you learn in a book. In your book, also:

• Tell about how heating and cooling are related.

• Tell about how addition and subtraction are related.

Name _____

# Review What You Know

### (A-Z) Vocabulary

1. Circle each **difference** in the math problems shown below.

   15 − 5 = 10

   ```
     23          14
   + 32         − 7
   ────        ────
     55           7
   ```

2. Circle the statement if it describes **mental math**.

   Math that is done with paper and pencil

   Math that you can do in your head

3. Circle the statement if it describes **compatible numbers**.

   Numbers that are close to numbers that you want to add or subtract

   Numbers that you can add or subtract using mental math

## Addition and Subtraction Facts

4. Complete the related addition and subtraction facts below.

   6 + ☐ = 13

   13 − ☐ = 6

5. Write each sum or difference.

   ```
     4      12       9      16
   + 7     − 3     + 6     − 8
   ───     ───     ───     ───
   ```

   *You can use addition facts to help you subtract.*

## Math Story

6. Tim has 25 stamps. Roy gives him 51 more stamps. How many stamps does Tim have now?

   _____ stamps

Topic 5

Name _____

**PROJECT 5A**

## How much does the largest gopher tortoise weigh?

**Project:** Write a Story About a Tortoise

**PROJECT 5B**

## How does the temperature change where you live?

**Project:** Create a Weather Report

**PROJECT 5C**

## How many moons do some planets in our solar system have?

**Project:** Research and Compare Moons

Before watching the video, think:

How do you help with laundry in your house? A great way to help the environment is to wash most of your laundry with cold water. The clothes still get clean, and you save up to 90 percent of the energy.

## I can ...

model with math to solve a problem that involves using strategies to subtract.

ⓒ **Mathematical Practices** MP.4
Also MP.2, MP.3
**Content Standards** 2.NBT.B.5
Also 2.OA.A.1, 2.NBT.B.9

Name _____

 Activity

**Solve & Share**

How can you use the hundred chart to help you find 57 – 23? Explain. Write an equation.

## Lesson 5-1

## Subtract Tens and Ones on a Hundred Chart

**I can …**
use a hundred chart to subtract tens and ones.

 **Content Standards** 2.NBT.B.5
Also 2.NBT.B.9
**Mathematical Practices** MP.3, MP.5, MP.7

| 1 | 2 | 3 | 4 | 5 | 6 | 7 | 8 | 9 | 10 |
|---|---|---|---|---|---|---|---|---|---|
| 11 | 12 | 13 | 14 | 15 | 16 | 17 | 18 | 19 | 20 |
| 21 | 22 | 23 | 24 | 25 | 26 | 27 | 28 | 29 | 30 |
| 31 | 32 | 33 | 34 | 35 | 36 | 37 | 38 | 39 | 40 |
| 41 | 42 | 43 | 44 | 45 | 46 | 47 | 48 | 49 | 50 |
| 51 | 52 | 53 | 54 | 55 | 56 | 57 | 58 | 59 | 60 |
| 61 | 62 | 63 | 64 | 65 | 66 | 67 | 68 | 69 | 70 |
| 71 | 72 | 73 | 74 | 75 | 76 | 77 | 78 | 79 | 80 |
| 81 | 82 | 83 | 84 | 85 | 86 | 87 | 88 | 89 | 90 |
| 91 | 92 | 93 | 94 | 95 | 96 | 97 | 98 | 99 | 100 |

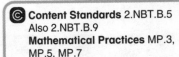

88 – 15 = __

57 ⊖ 23 = 34

Topic 5 | Lesson 1

Go Online | SavvasRealize.com

one hundred eighty-nine **189**

Find 43 – 28 using a hundred chart.

I can count back or count on to find the difference.

**One Way** Think: 43 – 28 = ?
Start at 43.
Count back 2 tens and 8 ones.
You land on 15.

| | | | | | | | | | |
|---|---|---|---|---|---|---|---|---|---|
| 11 | 12 | 13 | 14 | 15 | 16 | 17 | 18 | 19 | 20 |
| 21 | 22 | 23 | 24 | 25 | 26 | 27 | 28 | 29 | 30 |
| 31 | 32 | 33 | 34 | 35 | 36 | 37 | 38 | 39 | 40 |
| 41 | 42 | 43 | 44 | 45 | 46 | 47 | 48 | 49 | 50 |

So, 43 – 28 = 15.

**Another Way** Think: 28 + ? = 43
Start at 28. Count on to 43.

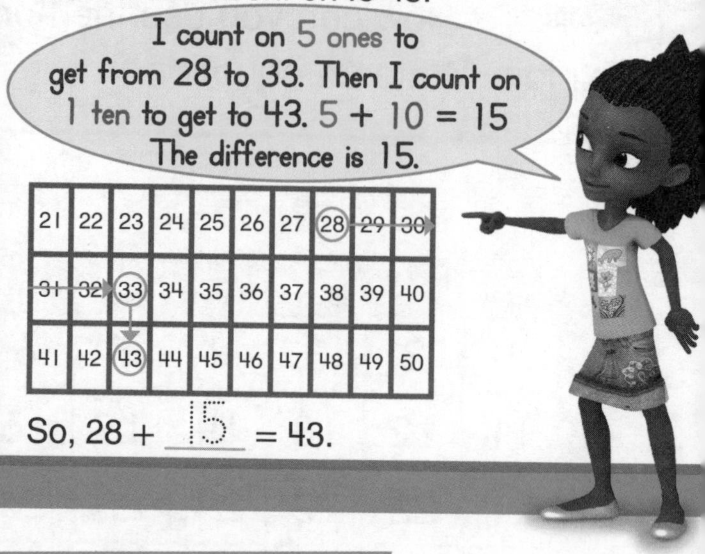
I count on 5 ones to get from 28 to 33. Then I count on 1 ten to get to 43. 5 + 10 = 15
The difference is 15.

| | | | | | | | | | |
|---|---|---|---|---|---|---|---|---|---|
| 21 | 22 | 23 | 24 | 25 | 26 | 27 | 28 | 29 | 30 |
| 31 | 32 | 33 | 34 | 35 | 36 | 37 | 38 | 39 | 40 |
| 41 | 42 | 43 | 44 | 45 | 46 | 47 | 48 | 49 | 50 |

So, 28 + 15 = 43.

**Convince Me!** How can you use a hundred chart to find 60 – 18?

**Guided Practice** Subtract using the hundred chart. Draw arrows if you need to.

| | | | | | | | | | |
|---|---|---|---|---|---|---|---|---|---|
| 21 | 22 | 23 | 24 | 25 | 26 | 27 | 28 | 29 | 30 |
| 31 | 32 | 33 | 34 | 35 | 36 | 37 | 38 | 39 | 40 |
| 41 | 42 | 43 | 44 | 45 | 46 | 47 | 48 | 49 | 50 |
| 51 | 52 | 53 | 54 | 55 | 56 | 57 | 58 | 59 | 60 |
| 61 | 62 | 63 | 64 | 65 | 66 | 67 | 68 | 69 | 70 |

1. 69 – 36 = 33

2. 54 – 24 = 30

3. 31 = 65 – 34

4. 47 – 22 = 25

Name Unarbek

**Solve & Share**

Jeremy had 56 bug stickers.
He gave 24 stickers to Eric.
How many bug stickers does Jeremy have left?
Use the open number line below to show your work.

**I can ...**
use an open number line to subtract tens and ones.

**Content Standards** 2.NBT.B.5
Also 2.NBT.B.9
**Mathematical Practices** MP.1,
MP.4, MP.5

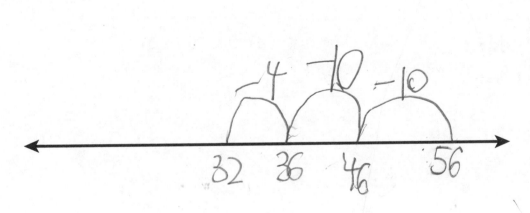

$$56 \ominus 24 = 32$$

Find 68 − 23.

Let's use an open number line and count back. First, place 68 on the line.

68

**One Way**
23 is 2 tens and 3 ones.
So, count back 2 tens from 68.
58, 48
Then, count back 3 ones from 48.
47, 46, 45

−1 −1 −1 −10 −10

45 46 47 48   58   68

**Another Way**
You can subtract 68 − **20** = 48,
then 48 − **3** = 45.

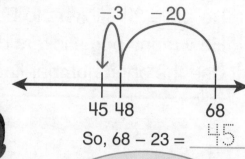

−3  −20

45 48   68

So, 68 − 23 = __45__.

I can check my subtraction by adding 45 + 23 = 68.

**Convince Me!** How can the open number line help you keep track as you count back?

☆**Guided Practice**☆ Use an open number line to find each difference.

**1.** 28 − 24 = __4__

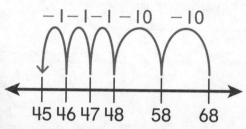

−4   −10   −10

4   8   18   28

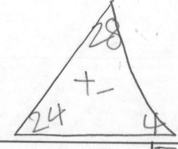
28
+−
24   4

**2.** 50 − 35 = __5__

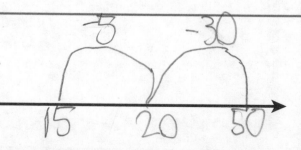

−5  −30

15   20   50

**Topic 5** | Lesson 2

Activity

**Solve & Share**

There are 50 children at the park. 28 are boys and the rest are girls. How many girls are at the park?

Use the open number line to solve. Show your work.

**I can ...**
add up to subtract using open number line.

© **Content Standards** 2.NBT.B.5
Also 2.NBT.B.9
**Mathematical Practices** MP.1, MP.2, MP.6

28

−8            − 20

22        30            50

$$50 \ominus 28 = 22$$

Visual Learning · A-Z Glossary

Find 57 – 28.

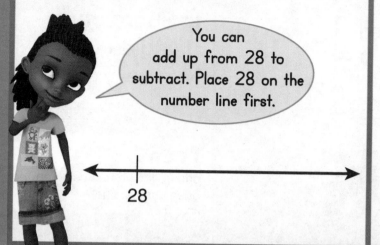

You can add up from 28 to subtract. Place 28 on the number line first.

28

You can add 2 to get to 30.

Then add 10, and 10 again, to get to 50.

Then add 7 to land on 57.

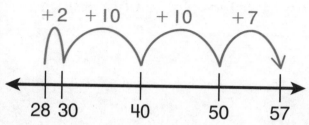

+2  +10  +10  +7

28 30  40  50  57

Add the tens and ones.

$2 + 10 + 10 + 7 = 29$

So, $57 – 28 = 29$.

I can check by adding! $28 + 29 = 57$

---

**Convince Me!** How can you add up to find 42 – 17?

☆ **Guided Practice** ☆ Add up to find each difference. Use an open number line.

1. $45 – 27 = \underline{18}$

45

+–

27          18

+3   +10   +5

27  30   40   45

2. $66 – 39 = \underline{27}$

66

+–

39    27

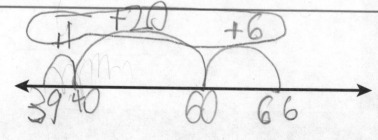

+1   +20   +6

39 40    60    66

**Topic 5** | Lesson 3

**Solve & Share**

Use any strategy to find 42 – 7.
Use pictures, words, or numbers to explain.

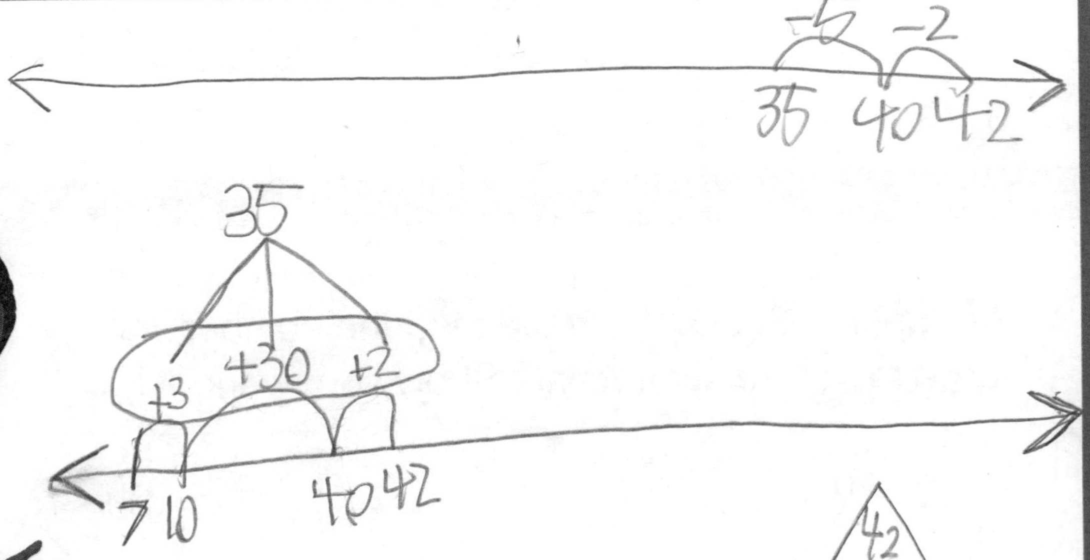

**I can ...**
break apart 1-digit numbers to help me subtract mentally.

**Content Standards** 2.NBT.B.5 Also 2.NBT.B.9
**Mathematical Practices** MP.3, MP.6, MP.7

−5  −2
35  40  42

35

+3  +30  +2

7 10    40 42

42 − 7 = $\underline{35}$  MN

42
+ _
7    35

$33 - 6 = ?$

You can break apart the number you are subtracting to find the difference.

Here are 3 ways to break apart 6. Which is best for subtracting 6 from 33?

6
1 + 5

6
2 + 4

6
3 + 3

$33 - 6 = \underline{\quad} ?$

3    3

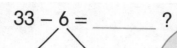
Start at 33. Subtract 3 to get to 30. Then subtract 3 more.

| 11 | 12 | 13 | 14 | 15 | 16 | 17 | 18 | 19 | 20 |
|----|----|----|----|----|----|----|----|----|----|
| 21 | 22 | 23 | 24 | 25 | 26 | 27 | 28 | 29 | 30 |
| 31 | 32 | 33 | 34 | 35 | 36 | 37 | 38 | 39 | 40 |

$33 - 6 = \underline{27}$

**Convince Me!** Look at the problem above. Why wasn't the 6 broken apart into $1 + 5$ to find $33 - 6$?

☆ **Guided Practice** ☆ Subtract. Break apart the number you are subtracting. Show your work.

1. $43 - 9 = \underline{\quad}$

3    6

2. $\underline{\quad} = 24 - 6$

4    2

| 11 | 12 | 13 | 14 | 15 | 16 | 17 | 18 | 19 | 20 |
|----|----|----|----|----|----|----|----|----|----|
| 21 | 22 | 23 | 24 | 25 | 26 | 27 | 28 | 29 | 30 |
| 31 | 32 | 33 | 34 | 35 | 36 | 37 | 38 | 39 | 40 |
| 41 | 42 | 43 | 44 | 45 | 46 | 47 | 48 | 49 | 50 |

**202** two hundred two

Activity

☆ Solve & Share ☆

Yuri wants to use mental math to find 86 − 29.
Show how Yuri could find the difference.
Explain how she could use mental math.

**I can ...**
make numbers that are easier to subtract, then use mental math to find the difference.

© **Content Standards** 2.NBT.B.5
Also 2.NBT.B.9
**Mathematical Practices** MP.1,
MP.4, MP.8

Go Online | SavvasRealize.com

43 − 18 = ?

You can use compensation to make numbers that are easier to subtract.

It is easier to subtract 20 than 18.

**One Way**
Change both addends by adding or subtracting the same amount. Then subtract using mental math.

$$43 \quad - \quad 18 \quad = \quad ?$$
$$\downarrow +2 \qquad \downarrow +2$$
$$45 \quad - \quad 20 \quad = \quad 25$$

So, 43   −   18   =   25.

**Another Way**
Add 2 to 18.
Then subtract using mental math.
Then add 2 to find the answer.

$$43 - 18 = ?$$
$$\downarrow +2$$
$$43 - 20 = 23$$
$$\downarrow +2$$

So, 43 − 18 = 25.

I subtracted 2 more than 18, so I need to add 2 to 23 to find the answer.

---

**Convince Me!** Marc says to find 61 − 13, it's easier to subtract 10 instead of 13. He says if you subtract 3 from 13 to get 10, you must subtract 3 more from your answer. Do you agree? Explain.

⭐**Guided Practice**⭐ Use compensation to make numbers that are easier to subtract. Then solve. Show your work.

1.   52   −   8   = __44__

  ↓ +2   ↓ +2

  54   −   10   = 44

2.   76   −   27   = __49__

  ↓ +3   ↓ +3

  79   −   30 = 49

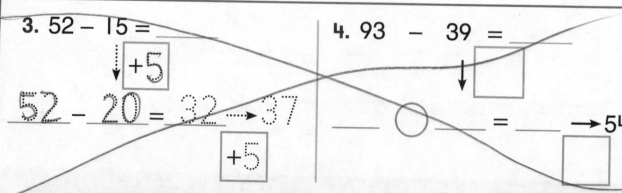

3. 52 − 15 = _____

  ↓ +5

  52 − 20 = 32 → 37

  +5

4. 93   −   39   = _____

  ↓

  _____   =   _____  → 54

**Topic 5** | Lesson 5

Name _____

**Solve & Share**

Randy got 42 craft sticks for a project. He used 19 sticks. How many sticks are left?

Choose any strategy. Solve. Show and explain your work.

**I can …**

choose a strategy to help me subtract two-digit numbers.

© **Content Standards** 2.NBT.B.5 Also 2.NBT.B.9 **Mathematical Practices** MP.2, MP.4, MP.5

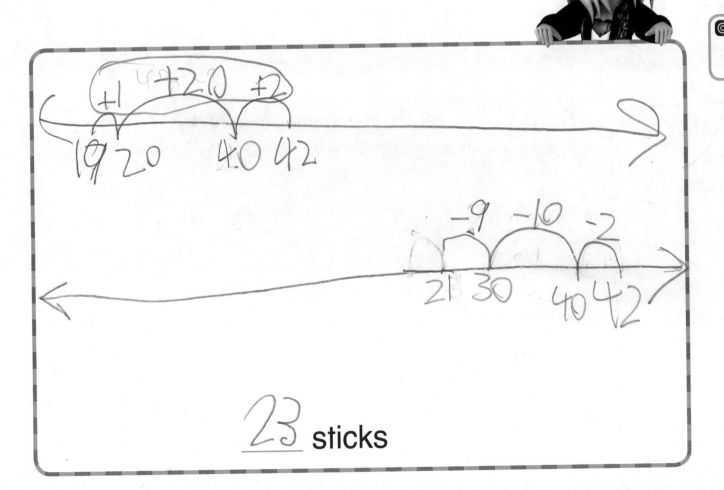

$\underline{23}$ sticks

Visual Learning
 A-Z Glossary

Find 65 – 37.

**One Way**

You can start at 37 and add up to 65. Count your moves to find the difference.

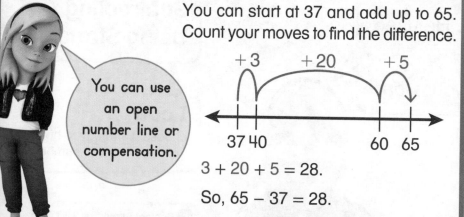

$+3$ $+20$ $+5$

37 40      60 65

$3 + 20 + 5 = 28.$

So, $65 - 37 = 28.$

You can use an open number line or compensation.

**Another Way**

You can use compensation.

$65 - 37$

$+3$

$65 - 40 = 25 \cdots\!\!\rightarrow 28$

$+3$

So, $65 - 37 = 28.$

You get the same answer both ways!

---

**Convince Me!** In **Another Way** above, why was 3 added to 37 and then added to 25?

☆ **Guided Practice** ☆ Find each difference. Use any strategy. Show your work.

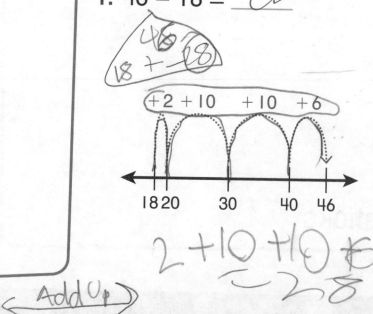

1. $46 - 18 =$ _28_

$+2 +10 +10 +6$

18 20    30    40 46

$2 + 10 + 10 + 6$
$= 28$

Add Up

2. $83 - 46 =$ _37_

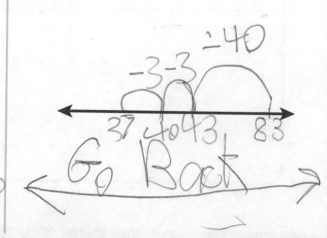

$-40$
$-3 -3$
37 40 43   83

Go Back

Name _____

**Solve & Share**

Some frogs were sitting on a pond.
16 more frogs joined them.
Now there are 49 frogs on the pond.
How many frogs were on the pond at first?
Show how you know.

### Solve One-Step and Two-Step Problems

**I can ...**
solve one- and two-step problems using addition or subtraction.

**Content Standards** 2.OA.A.1
Also 2.NBT.B.5
**Mathematical Practices** MP.1,
MP.2, MP.4

Matt has 8 game cards.
He wins 7 more cards.
Then he gives José 4 cards.
How many cards does Matt have now?

You can use bar diagrams to help solve each step.

**Step 1**
Find the number of cards after Matt wins 7.

$8 + 7 = 15$
Matt has 15 cards.

**Step 2**
Find the number of cards after Matt gives away 4.

$15 - 4 = 11$
Matt has 11 cards now.

Check that your answer makes sense.

Matt had 8 game cards.
He won 7 more cards.
Then he gave José 4 cards.
Now he has 11 cards.

$8 + 7 = 15$
$15 - 4 = 11$

My answer makes sense!

---

**Convince Me!** Cory scored some points. Then he scored 8 more points. He scored 14 points in all. How many points did Cory score at first? How can you solve the problem?

☆ **Guided Practice** ☆ Complete both equations to solve the problem. Use the bar diagram to help you.

1. Some people got on the bus at the first stop.
9 more people got on the bus at the second stop.
There are 21 people on the bus now.
How many people got on the bus at the first stop?

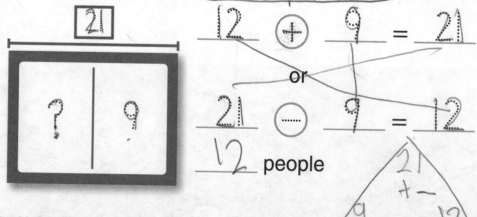

$\underline{12} \underline{\oplus} \underline{9} = \underline{21}$

or

$\underline{21} \underline{\ominus} \underline{9} = \underline{12}$

$\underline{12}$ people

Name _____

**Solve & Share**

Bill collects and sells seashells. He has 45 shells, finds 29 shells, and sells 20 shells. How many seashells does Bill have now?

Tara says you have to subtract 45 − 29 and then add 20 to solve the problem. Do you agree with Tara's thinking? Circle your answer. Use pictures, words, or equations to explain.

$45 + 29 = 74$
$74 + 20 = 54$

**I can ...**
critique the thinking of others by using what I know about addition and subtraction.

© **Mathematical Practices** MP.3
Also MP.1, MP.4, MP.7
**Content Standards** 2.NBT.B.9
Also 2.OA.A.1, 2.NBT.B.5

**Agree**          **Do Not Agree**

Because ↓

**Thinking Habits**

What questions can I ask to understand other people's thinking?

Are there mistakes in other people's thinking?

42 people are swimming. Some people leave. Now 15 people are swimming.

Kelly added up to subtract. She says 17 people left.

**How can I decide if I agree with Kelly?**

I can check for mistakes or ask Kelly questions.

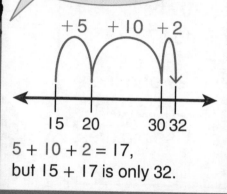

I can draw a number line and add up to check for mistakes.

$+5$  $+10$  $+2$

15  20  30  32

$5 + 10 + 2 = 17$,
but $15 + 17$ is only 32.

Kelly's strategy of adding up is good, but her answer is not correct.

$+5$  $+10$  $+10$  $+2$

15  20  30  40  42

$15 + 27 = 42$
So, 27 people left.

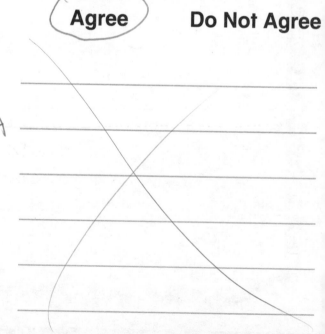

---

**Convince Me!** What question would you ask Kelly to help her check her reasoning?

☆ **Guided Practice** ☆ Circle your answer. Use pictures, words, or equations to explain your reasoning.

1. 51 people were on a train. 33 people left the train. How many people are on the train now?

Ryan says 18 people. He broke apart 33 into 30 and 3. Then he subtracted each number. Does Ryan's reasoning make sense?

(Agree)    **Do Not Agree**

Name _____

Find a partner. Point to a clue. Read the clue.

Look below the clues to find a match. Write the clue letter in the box next to the match.

Find a match for every clue.

**I can ...**
add and subtract within 20.

© **Content Standard** 2.OA.B.2
**Mathematical Practices** MP.3, MP.6, MP.7, MP.8

**Clues**

**A** Every difference is 10.

**B** Every sum is 11.

**C** Every sum and difference is 6.

**D** Exactly three sums are the same.

**E** Exactly three differences are the same.

**F** Every sum is the same as 9 + 4.

**G** Every difference is odd.

**H** Exactly three sums are even.

| | | | |
|---|---|---|---|
| ☐ 12 − 5<br>17 − 8<br>14 − 7<br>16 − 9 | ☐ 10 − 0<br>20 − 10<br>14 − 4<br>19 − 9 | ☐ 6 + 6<br>2 + 8<br>7 + 4<br>5 + 7 | ☐ 14 − 8<br>3 + 3<br>15 − 9<br>0 + 6 |
| ☐ 8 + 6<br>7 + 8<br>9 + 6<br>10 + 5 | ☐ 15 − 8<br>18 − 9<br>12 − 7<br>13 − 6 | ☐ 5 + 6<br>4 + 7<br>9 + 2<br>3 + 8 | ☐ 7 + 6<br>3 + 10<br>8 + 5<br>4 + 9 |

A-Z
Glossary

## Word List
- break apart
- compatible numbers
- compensation
- difference
- mental math
- ones
- open number line
- tens

## Understand Vocabulary

Choose a term from the Word List to complete each sentence.

1. You can count back or add up to subtract on an

   _____.

2. To find 42 – 7, you can _____ 7 into 2 + 5.

3. The answer to a subtraction problem is called the _____.

4. There are 6 _____ in the number 36.

5. In 43, there are _____ tens.

6. In 76, there are _____ tens and _____ ones.

7. Break apart 8 to find 65 – 8.

   _____

## Use Vocabulary in Writing

8. Use words to tell how to find 54 – 19. Use terms from the Word List.

**Set A**

You can use a hundred chart to help you subtract. Find 65 − 31.

Start at 31. Move right 4 ones to 35.
Then move down 3 tens to 65.
3 tens and 4 ones is 34.

So, 65 − 31 = __34__.

| | | | | | | | | | |
|---|---|---|---|---|---|---|---|---|---|
| ③① | 32 | 33 | 34 | ㉟ | 36 | 37 | 38 | 39 | 40 |
| 41 | 42 | 43 | 44 | 45 | 46 | 47 | 48 | 49 | 50 |
| 51 | 52 | 53 | 54 | 55 | 56 | 57 | 58 | 59 | 60 |
| 61 | 62 | 63 | 64 | ⑥⑤ | 66 | 67 | 68 | 69 | 70 |

Use a hundred chart to solve the problems.

1. 67 − 42 = __25__

2. 70 − 33 = __37__

3. 58 − 42 = __16__

4. 63 − 38 = __25__

**Set B**

You can use an open number line to find 57 − 24.

Place 57 on the number line. 24 is 2 tens and 4 ones. So, you can count back by 10 two times. Then count back 4.

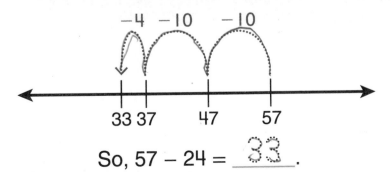

So, 57 − 24 = __33__.

Use an open number line to find each difference.

5. 38 − 13 = __25__

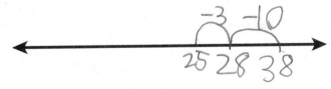

6. 93 − 36 = __57__

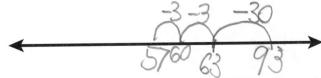

Find 62 – 37.

Place 37 on the line. Then add up to 62. You can add 3 to get to 40. Then add two 10s to get to 60. Then add 2 to get to 62. Add the jumps of tens and ones: 3 + 10 + 10 + 2 = 25.

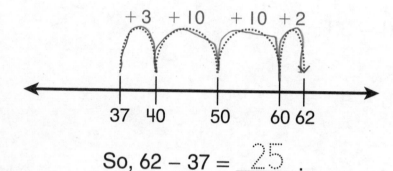

So, 62 – 37 = 25 .

Add up on an open number line to find each difference.

**7.** 75 – 47 = 28

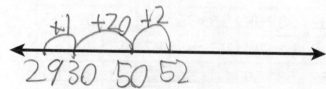

**8.** 52 – 29 = 23

+1   +20   +2
29 30   50 52

Break apart 7 to find 54 – 7.

54 – 7

4   3

Start at 54. Subtract 4. Then subtract 3 more.
So, 54 – 7 = 47 .

Subtract. Break apart the number you are subtracting. Show your work.

**9.** 52 – 6 = 46

50 2

**10.** 45 – 9 = 56

Name _____

## Set E

74 − 27 = ?

Use compensation to solve.

$$74 - 27$$
$$\downarrow +3$$
$$74 - 30 = 44 \dashrightarrow 47$$
$$+3$$

So, 74 − 27 = __47__ .

| Use compensation to subtract. | **Reteaching** Continued |

11. 42 − 18 = _____

12. 84 − 37 = _____

## Set F

You can use different strategies and tools to subtract.

For example, you can:

- use a __hundred__ chart.

- count back or __add up__ on an open number line.

- break apart the number
  you are __subtracting__ .

- use compensation to make an easier problem.

| Use any strategy to solve the problem. Show your work. |

13. Lily has a puzzle with 8 fewer pieces than Jake has. Jake has 45 pieces. How many pieces does Lily have?

_____ pieces

Use the bar diagram and write two equations to model and solve the problem.

Mason read 34 pages in two days. He read 8 pages on Day 1. How many pages did he read on Day 2?

26 + 8 = 34 and
34 − 8 = 26

<u>26</u> pages

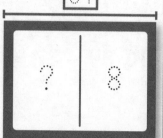

Add or subtract to solve the problem. Show your work.

14. Gene bakes 60 muffins in one day. He bakes 24 of the muffins before lunch. How many muffins does he bake after lunch?

____ ◯ ____ = ____

____ muffins

### Thinking Habits

**Critique Reasoning**

What questions can I ask to understand other people's thinking?

Are there mistakes in other people's thinking?

Do you agree or disagree? Explain.

15. Ken has 29 more stamps than Jamie. Ken has 52 stamps. Lisa says Jamie has 23 stamps.

Lisa added up 1 from 29, then 20 more from 30, and 2 more to get to 52. Does Lisa's reasoning make sense?

**9.** The number line below shows adding up to subtract to find 68 − 36. What is the difference? Explain how you know.

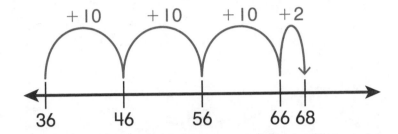

**10.** Use the open number line to find the difference.

$$80 - 42 = ?$$

$$80 - 42 = \underline{\hspace{1cm}}$$

**11. A.** 33 ants are on a leaf. 15 ants leave. How many ants are left?
Jay adds 2 to 33 to make an easier problem, 35 − 15. He says 20 ants are left. Circle whether you agree or do not agree.

**Agree**          **Do Not Agree**

**B.** Explain why you agree or do not agree with Jay's strategy.

_____

_____

_____

_____

**12.** Use the open number lines. Show two different ways to find 74 – 28. Show your work.

**One Way**

74 – 28 = _____

**Another Way**

74 – 28 = _____

**13.** Use the numbers on the cards. Write the missing numbers to solve the problem. What strategy did you use to solve the problem? Explain.

| 3 | 35 | 40 | 75 |

72  –  37  =  _____

+3        ☐ +

_____ – _____ = _____

**14.** 5 black cows are at the ranch.
9 brown cows join them.
Then 6 cows leave the ranch.
How many cows are still at the ranch?

Solve. Show your work.

| Step 1 |
|---|
| Step 2 |
| Answer |
| _____ cows |

Name _____

## Beautiful Boats

Chen's family goes to the lake for a vacation.
They count the boats that they see.

2 sailboats          28 rowboats          36 motorboats

1. How many more motorboats does
   Chen see than sailboats?

   Use the open number line to
   solve.

_____ more motorboats

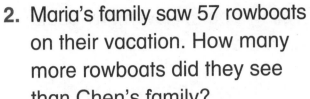
2. Maria's family saw 57 rowboats
   on their vacation. How many
   more rowboats did they see
   than Chen's family?

   Use compensation to solve.
   Explain how you found your answer.

   _____ more rowboats

**3.** Chen's sisters have toy boats. They have 21 yellow boats. They have 9 fewer red boats than yellow boats. How many boats do they have in all?

Choose any strategy. Show your work.

_____ boats

**4.** Julie's family saw 94 boats on their vacation. How many more boats did they see than Chen's family?

**Part A** What do you need to do to solve the problem?

**Part B** How many boats did Chen see? Show your work. Then explain how you found your answer.

_____ boats

**Part C** Julie said that her family saw 18 more boats than Chen's family. She broke apart 76 into 70 + 4 + 2. Then she subtracted each number from 94. Does Julie's reasoning make sense? Explain.

## TOPIC 6
# Fluently Subtract Within 100

**Essential Question:** What are strategies for subtracting numbers to 100?

More of Earth is covered with water than with land!

And some of the land is covered with snow and ice!

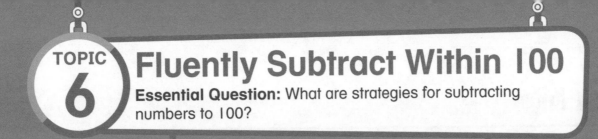

Wow! Let's do this project and learn more.

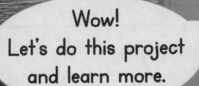

**enVision** STEM Project: Finding Water and Finding Differences

**Find Out** Use globes, maps, books, and other sources to find out where water, snow, and ice can be found on Earth. Make a list of different names of bodies of water and names of bodies of snow and ice.

**Journal: Make a Book** Show what you learn in a book. In your book, also:

• Tell about how globes are models that show where water is found on Earth.

• Tell about how to use a subtraction model to find differences.

Name _____

## A-Z Vocabulary

**1. Break apart** 56 into tens and ones. Draw place value blocks to show the parts.

56 = _____ + _____

**2.** Complete the drawing to show how to **regroup** 1 ten as ones.

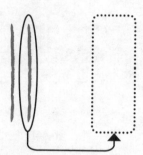

**3.** Complete the **bar diagram** to model 64 − 31 = ?

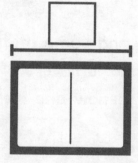

## Open Number Lines

**4.** Find 40 − 25 by counting back on an open number line. Show your work.

40 − 25 = _____

**5.** Find 45 − 22 by adding up on an open number line. Show your work.

45 − 22 = _____

## Math Story

**6.** Lea has 30 cookies. She gives 17 cookies to her friends. How many cookies does Lea have now?

_____ cookies

**234** two hundred thirty-four

Topic 6

Name _____

**PROJECT 6A**

## Do snakes lay eggs?

**Project:** Make a Model of a Snake and Its Nest

**PROJECT 6B**

## How are schools different around the world?

**Project:** Compare and Contrast Classroom Sizes

**Topic 6** | Pick a Project

## PROJECT 6C

### How long does it take to drive from a large city to nearby places?

**Project:** Draw a Map of Some State Places

## PROJECT 6D

### What stories are in the night sky?

**Project:** Perform a Skit About Constellations

Activity

**Solve & Share**

How can you use tens and ones to find 23 – 6?
Use place-value blocks to help you. Show your work.

**I can ...**
use place value and models to subtract 1-digit numbers.

© **Content Standards** 2.NBT.B.5
Also 2.NBT.B.9
**Mathematical Practices** MP.1,
MP.3, MP.5

_____ – _____ = _____

Go Online | SavvasRealize.com

Find 34 − 6. Use place-value blocks.

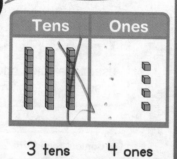

Show 34 with tens and ones.

| Tens | Ones |
|------|------|

3 tens    4 ones

**One Way**
Take away 4 ones.
Regroup 1 ten as 10 ones.
Take away 2 more ones.

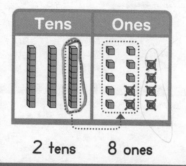

| Tens | Ones |
|------|------|

2 tens    8 ones

**Another Way**
Regroup 1 ten as
10 ones first.
Then take away 6 ones.

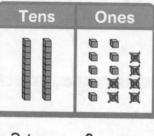

| Tens | Ones |
|------|------|

2 tens    8 ones

Cross out 6 ones. Now there are 2 tens and 8 ones left. This shows the difference.

So, 34 − 6 = __28__.

**Convince Me!** In the first example above, why were 4 ones taken away first?

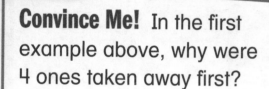 **Guided Practice**  Subtract. Use place-value blocks. Draw blocks to show your work.

1. 63 − 2 = 61

| Tens | Ones |
|------|------|

2. 44 − 9 = 35

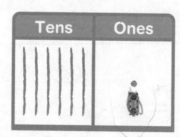

| Tens | Ones |
|------|------|

3. 32 − 8 = ___

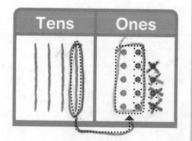

| Tens | Ones |
|------|------|

**Topic 6 | Lesson**

Name _____

**Solve & Share**

You have 42 pipe cleaners.
You use 19 of the pipe cleaners.
How many pipe cleaners do you have now?

Use place-value blocks to help you solve.
Draw place-value blocks to show your work.

**I can …**
use place value and models to
subtract 2-digit numbers.

**Content Standards** 2.NBT.B.5
Also 2.NBT.B.9
**Mathematical Practices** MP.3,
MP.4, MP.7

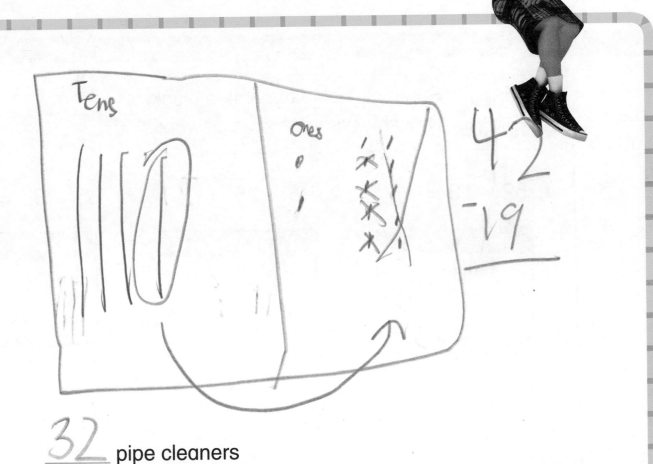

Tens    Ones

42
-19

32 pipe cleaners

Find 43 − 24. Use place-value blocks.

**One Way**
Take away 2 tens 3 ones.

Regroup 1 ten as 10 ones.
Take away 1 more.

 Show 43 with tens and ones.

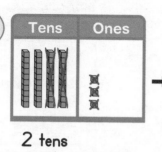

2 tens

1 ten   9 ones
So, 43 − 24 = 19.

**Another Way**
Take away 2 tens.

Regroup 1 ten as 10 ones.
Take away 4 ones.

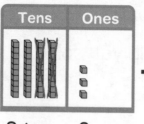

2 tens   3 ones

1 ten   9 ones
So, 43 − 24 = 19.

 There are many ways to subtract.

**Convince Me!** How are the two ways shown above alike? How are they different?

**Guided Practice** Subtract. Use place-value blocks. Draw blocks to show your work.

**1.** 52 − 13 = 39

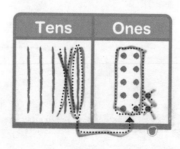

**2.** 46 − 25 = 21

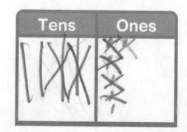

**3.** 65 − 37 = 28

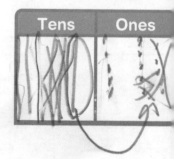

**Topic 6** | Lesson 2

Activity

**Solve & Share**

Ari has 72 stickers. He puts 25 of his stickers in a scrapbook. How many stickers are left?

Draw place-value blocks to help you solve the problem.

**I can ...**
subtract using place value and partial differences.

© **Content Standards** 2.NBT.B.5 Also 2.OA.A.1, 2.NBT.B.9 **Mathematical Practices** MP.2, MP.4, MP.5

Find 64 – 36.
You can use place-value blocks to subtract and record **partial differences**.

**What You Show**

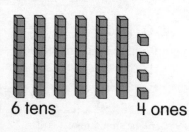

6 tens    4 ones

You can subtract 3 tens from 6 tens.

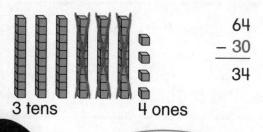

3 tens     4 ones

$$\begin{array}{r}64\\-30\\\hline34\end{array}$$

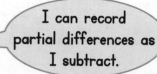

I can record partial differences as I subtract.

Subtract 6 ones.
First, subtract 4 ones to make a 10.

Regroup 1 ten as 10 ones.
Then subtract 2 ones.

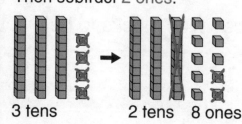

3 tens    2 tens   8 ones

$$\begin{array}{r}64\\-30\\\hline34\\-4\\\hline30\\-2\\\hline28\end{array}$$

So, 64 – 36 = __28__ .

**Convince Me!** The example above shows one way to find 64 – 36 using partial differences. Could you begin by subtracting the ones instead of the tens? Explain.

**Guided Practice** Subtract. Use place-value blocks to find partial differences. Record your work.

1.   34 – 15 = _____

$$\begin{array}{r}34\\-10\\\hline24\\-4\\\hline20\\-1\end{array}$$

Subtract 1 ten.
Subtract 4 ones.
Subtract 1.

2.   63 – 48 = _____

$$\begin{array}{r}63\\-3\\\hline60\\-5\\\hline55\\-40\end{array}$$

Subtract 3 ones.
Subtract 5 ones.
Subtract 4 tens.

**Independent Practice**  Subtract. Use place-value blocks to find partial differences. Record your work.

**3.**  52 – 36 = _____

**4.**  94 – 54 = _____

**5.**  41 – 25 = _____

**6.**  33 – 28 = _____

**7.**  65 – 42 = _____

**8.**  70 – 48 = _____

**9.**  96 – 37 = _____

**10.**  87 – 45 = _____

Solve. Draw a model to help.

**11. Higher Order Thinking** Tia's basketball team scored 61 points. They won by 23 points. How many points did the other team score?

_____ points

**12. Model** Don has 72 marbles. Josie has 56 marbles. How many more marbles does Don have than Josie?

Can you use drawings of place-value blocks to show partial differences?

_____ more marbles

**13. Higher Order Thinking** Write a subtraction story using two 2-digit numbers. Then solve the problem in your story.

_____

_____

_____

_____

_____

_____

**14.** ☑ **Assessment Practice** Which numbers will complete this partial differences problem for 44 − 17?

Choose all that apply.

$$
\begin{array}{r}
44 \\
-10 \\
\hline
? \\
-4 \\
\hline
? \\
-3 \\
\hline
27
\end{array}
$$

☐ 20

☐ 30

☐ 31

☐ 34

Activity

**Continue to Subtract Using Partial Differences**

Solve & Share

Show two different ways to find 53 – 28.

**I can ...**
use partial differences and mentally break apart the number I am subtracting.

© **Content Standards** 2.NBT.B.5
Also 2.NBT.B.9
**Mathematical Practices** MP.1,
MP.2, MP.3

Find 81 – 27.

You know how to count back on a number line to subtract.

*Think about place value!*

You can also mentally break apart the number you are subtracting.

81 – 27 = ?

```
        20        7
               /     \
             1        6
```

You can record partial differences.

```
   81
 – 20
 ────
   61
 –  1
 ────
   60
 –  6
 ────
   54
```

*Here's one way to record.*

So, 81 – 27 = __54__.

---

**Convince Me!** Find 73 – 45. Andy says he can subtract 3, then 2, and then 40 to find the difference. Do you agree? Explain.

☆ **Guided Practice** ☆ Subtract. Use partial differences. Break apart the number you are subtracting. Show your work.

1. 54 – 26 = _____

```
        20        6
               /     \
             4
```

```
  54
– 20
────
```

2. 43 – 18 = _____

```
      □        □
           /     \
         □        □
```

Tools  Assessment

**Independent Practice**  Subtract. Use partial differences. Break apart the number you are subtracting. Show your work.

3. _____ = 32 – 13

4. 74 – 28 = _____

5. _____ = 61 – 47

6. 84 – 46 = _____

7. 59 – 17 = _____

8. _____ = 95 – 38

9. **Higher Order Thinking** Tina found 53 – 27 by breaking apart 27 into 23 and 4. Does Tina's way work?

Show another way you could break apart 27 to find 53 – 27. Then find the difference.

10. **enVision® STEM** Kate had 32 ice cubes. She put 14 of them in the sun and they melted. How many ice cubes does Kate have now?

_____ ice cubes

11. **Make Sense** Mark has 27 stamps. Sam has 82 stamps. Lena has 42 stamps. How many more stamps does Sam have than Mark?

> Think about what you know and what you need to find.

_____ more stamps

12. **Higher Order Thinking** Allison found 51 − 34 using partial differences. She broke apart 34 into 31 + 3.

Write equations to show how Allison could have found the difference.

13. ☑ **Assessment Practice** Can you use the equations to find 63 − 45? Choose Yes or No.

63 − 3 = 60
60 − 2 = 58        ○ Yes    ○ No
58 − 40 = 18

63 − 40 = 23      ○ Yes    ○ No
23 − 5 = 18

45 − 10 = 35      ○ Yes    ○ No
35 − 5 = 30

Activity

**Solve & Share**

Find 82 – 56. Use any strategy you have learned or your own strategy. Show your work. Explain why your strategy works.

## I can ...

subtract 2-digit numbers using any strategy I've learned and explain why the strategy works.

© **Content Standards** 2.NBT.B.5 Also 2.NBT.B.9
**Mathematical Practices** MP.1, MP.2, MP.6

Go Online | SavvasRealize.com

Find 72 − 24.
**One way** is to draw blocks, regroup, subtract, and record partial differences.

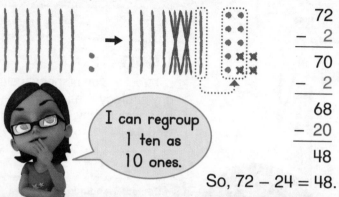

I can regroup 1 ten as 10 ones.

$$72$$
$$- \ 2$$
$$\overline{70}$$
$$- \ 2$$
$$\overline{68}$$
$$- 20$$
$$\overline{48}$$

So, 72 − 24 = 48.

**Another way** is to break apart numbers, subtract, and record partial differences.

72 − 24 = ?

20   4

2   2

$$72$$
$$- 20$$
$$\overline{52}$$
$$- \ 2$$
$$\overline{50}$$
$$- \ 2$$
$$\overline{48}$$

So, 72 − 24 = 48.

You can explain why a subtraction strategy works.

Partial differences works! The ones and tens I subtract equal 24, the number I am subtracting.

**Convince Me!** Could you solve 72 − 24 using a different strategy? Explain.

★ **Guided Practice** ★   Use any strategy to subtract. Show your work. Draw blocks if needed. Explain why the strategy works.

**1.** 67 − 39 = _____

67 − 40 = 27
27 + 1 = 28

Compensation works. It is easy to subtract 40, but I have to add 1 to the difference.

**2.** 78 − 42 = _____

## Independent Practice

Use any strategy to subtract. Show your work.
Be ready to explain why your strategy works.

**3.** 73 – 4 = _____

**4.** 78 – 25 = _____

**5.** 83 – 46 = _____

**6.** 36 – 27 = _____

**7.** 98 – 51 = _____

**8.** 65 – 7 = _____

**9.** 86 – 19 = _____

**10.** 71 – 8 = _____

**11.** 85 – 23 = _____

**Algebra** Find the missing number.

**12.** 34 – 8 = 35 – ☐

**13.** 27 – 9 = 28 – ☐

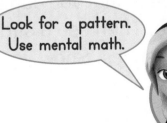

Look for a pattern.
Use mental math.

**14.** A hardware store has 32 hammers in stock. The store sells 16 hammers on Saturday. How many hammers are left?

_____ hammers

**15.** A barber does 15 haircuts on Monday. He does 28 haircuts on Friday. How many more haircuts does he do on Friday than on Monday?

_____ more haircuts

**16.** (A-Z) **Vocabulary** Complete each sentence. Use two of the words below.

**addend    equation    difference    sum**

$93 - 53 = 40$ is an _____.

40 is called the _____ of 93 and 53.

**17. Higher Order Thinking** Fill in the missing digits of this subtraction problem.

$$\boxed{\phantom{0}}\,\boxed{\phantom{0}} - 23 = 29$$

**18.** ☑ **Assessment Practice** Circle the problem that you can use regrouping to solve. Then use a strategy to find both differences. Show your work.

$56 - 38 =$ _____        $74 - 52 =$ _____

Name _____

**Solve & Share**

Trevor made 20 apple muffins for the bake sale. Ryan made 15 banana muffins. They sold 23 muffins in all. How many muffins are left to sell?

Solve any way you choose. Show your work.

**I can ...**
use models and equations to solve word problems.

© **Content Standards** 2.OA.A.1
Also 2.NBT.B.5
**Mathematical Practices** MP.1, MP.2, MP.4

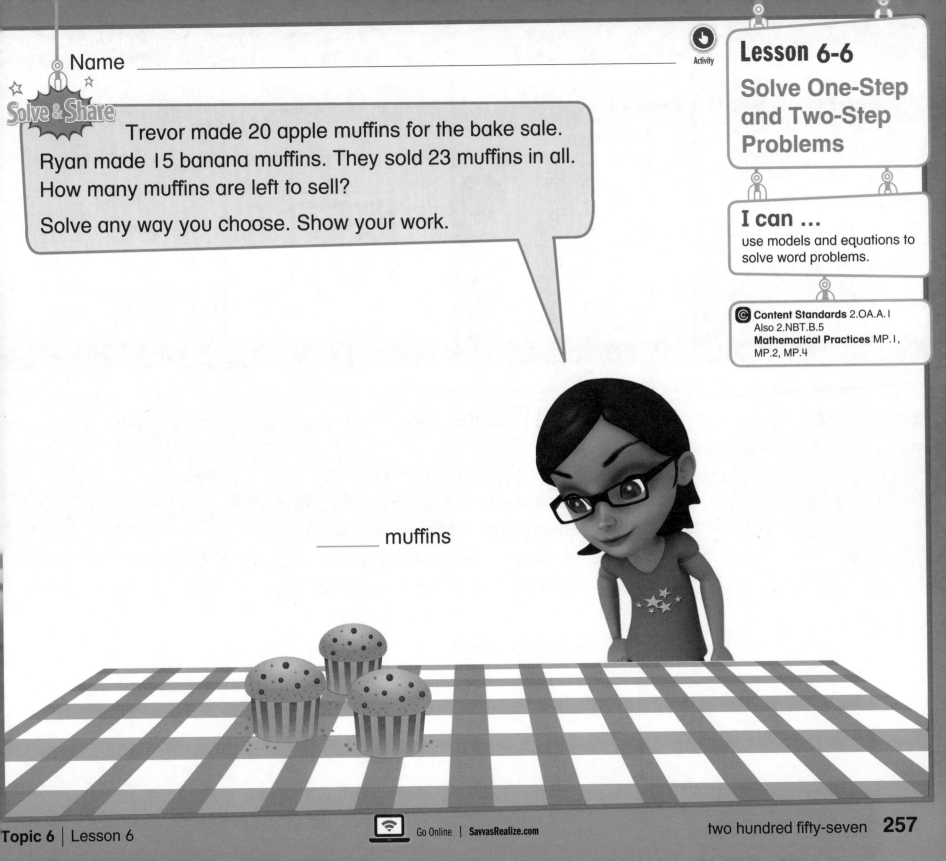

_____ muffins

Some students are in the gym. 13 students leave. Now there are 15 students in the gym.

How many students were in the gym at the start?

What is happening in the story?

You can write an equation. First, think about what you need to find.

*How many students were in the gym at the start?*

You can use a ? for the unknown.

$? - 13 = 15$

You can also use a bar diagram to show the parts and the whole.

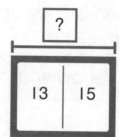

| ? | |
|---|---|
| 13 | 15 |

You can add the parts to find the unknown total.

13
+ 15
———
Tens: 20
Ones: + 8
———
Sum: 28

So, 28 students were in the gym at the start.

**Convince Me!** Look at the example above. How does the bar diagram show that you can add to find the answer?

⭐ **Guided Practice**   Solve the problem. Show your work.

1. Kyla's goal is to walk her dog 50 blocks on Friday, Saturday, and Sunday. On Friday, she walked 16 blocks. On Saturday, she walked 18 blocks. How many blocks does she need to walk on Sunday to meet her goal?

**Step 1:**

$16 \oplus 18 = 34$

**Step 2:**

$50 \ominus 34 = 16$

_____ blocks

**Independent Practice**  Use a bar diagram to solve each problem. Show your work.

**2.** Some balls are in the closet. Mr. Thomas takes out 15 balls for class. Now there are 56 balls in the closet. How many balls were in the closet in the beginning?

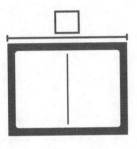

_____ balls

**3.** Corey buys a box of 96 paper clips from the store. He uses 34 paper clips. How many paper clips does Corey have left?

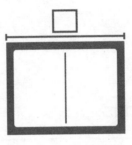

_____ paper clips

**4.** A.J. counts 44 acorns in his yard. He picks up 27 acorns. Then 16 more acorns fall from the tree. How many acorns are in the yard now? Show your work.

Think about what to find first. Then use that answer to solve the problem.

**Step 1:**

_____ ◯ _____ = _____

**Step 2:**

_____ ◯ _____ = _____

_____ acorns

## Problem Solving

**Make Sense** Make a plan. Solve each problem.
Show your work. Then check your work.

5. 27 people are at a picnic. 14 people eat hamburgers. The rest eat hot dogs. How many people eat hot dogs?

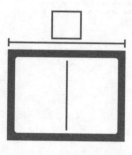

_____ people eat hot dogs

6. Some pumpkins are in a patch. 41 pumpkins are picked. Now there are 33 pumpkins in the patch. How many pumpkins were in the patch at the start?

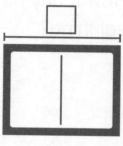

_____ pumpkins

7. **Higher Order Thinking** Lauren has a stamp collection. She gives Kristen 12 stamps and Ethan 15 stamps. Lauren has 22 stamps left. How many stamps did she have at the start?

**Step 1:**

**Step 2:**

_____ ◯ _____ = _____

_____ stamps

8. ☑ **Assessment Practice** Lance buys 48 eggs. He uses 24 of them for baking. Then he buys 12 more eggs. How many eggs does Lance have now?

Which set of equations can you use to solve this problem?

Ⓐ $48 + 24 = 72$
$72 - 12 = 60$

Ⓒ $48 + 24 = 72$
$72 + 12 = 84$

Ⓑ $48 - 24 = 24$
$24 + 12 = 36$

Ⓓ $48 - 24 = 24$
$24 - 12 = 12$

Name _____

**Solve & Share**

Farmer Davis has 52 chickens. Farmer Phil has 15 fewer chickens. How many chickens does Farmer Phil have?

Do you add or subtract to solve this problem? Explain why. Solve. Show your work.

**I can ...**
reason about word problems, and use bar diagrams and equations to solve them.

© **Mathematical Practices** MP.2
Also MP.1, MP.4, MP.5, MP.6
**Content Standards** 2.OA.A.1
Also 2.NBT.B.9

### Thinking Habits
How are the numbers in the problem related?

How can I show a word problem using pictures or numbers?

45 beads are in a jar. Jenny uses some beads to make a necklace. Now 17 beads are in the jar.

How many beads does Jenny use to make the necklace?

**How can I use reasoning to solve the problem?**

45 beads – beads in = 17 beads
necklace    left

 I can think about how the numbers are related. 45 – ? = 17 A bar diagram can show this.

I know the whole. So, I can subtract the part I know to find the missing part.

45
? | 17

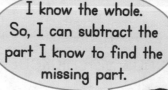

Find 45 – 17 = ?.

$$
\begin{array}{r}
45 \\
- 10 \\
\hline
35 \\
- 5 \\
\hline
30 \\
- 2 \\
\hline
28
\end{array}
$$

45 – 17 = 28 beads

My bar diagram and equation show how the numbers relate.

---

**Convince Me!** Why can you subtract 45 – 17 to solve 45 – ? = 17?

☆ **Guided Practice** ☆  Reason about the numbers in each problem. Complete the bar diagram and write an equation to solve. Show your work.

1. Wendy has 38 cents to spend on a snack. She buys an apple that costs 22 cents. How many cents does Wendy have left?

 38 ⊖ 22 ⊜ _____ cents

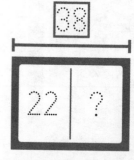
38
22 | ?

2. Joe has 46 crayons. Tamila has 18 more crayons than Joe. How many crayons does Tamila have?

_____ ◯ _____ ◯ _____ crayons

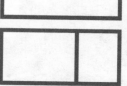

**Topic 6 | Lesson 7**

Tools   Assessment

☆**ndependent** **Reason about how the numbers in each problem relate. Complete**
**☆ Practice** **the bar diagram and write an equation to solve. Show your work.**

3. **enVision**® **STEM** Andy's class wants to test samples of river water. They want to test 47 water samples. So far, they tested 34 samples. How many more samples do they need to test?

_____ ◯ _____ ◯ _____ more samples

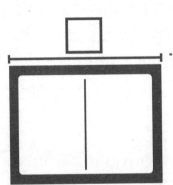

4. 93 dimes are in a box. Grant uses some to buy a game. Now, 66 dimes are in the box. How many dimes did Grant use to buy the game?

_____ ◯ _____ ◯ _____ dimes

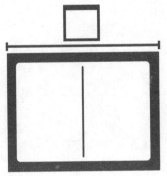

5. Maria paints 62 squares for a mural. Oscar paints 38 squares. How many more squares does Maria paint than Oscar?

_____ ◯ _____ ◯ _____ more squares

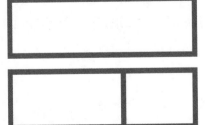

# Problem Solving

## Planting Trees

The second- and third-grade students planted these trees in Wing Park. The second-grade students planted 26 of the spruce trees. How many spruce trees did the third-grade students plant?

**38 Oak**    **44 Spruce**

**6. Make Sense** What information can you get from the pictures?

_____

_____

_____

_____

**7. Model** Complete the bar diagram. Decide how the numbers in the problem relate. Then write an equation that shows how to solve the problem.

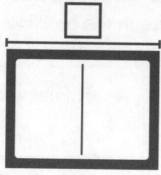

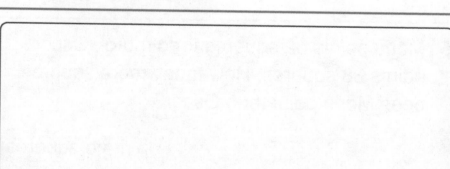

**8. Reasoning** How many spruce trees did the third-grade students plant? Explain how you solved the problem.

_____ spruce trees

Name _____

**Point & Tally**

Find a partner. Get paper and a pencil. Each partner chooses a different color: light blue or dark blue.

Partner 1 and Partner 2 each point to a black number at the same time. Both partners add those numbers.

If the answer is on your color, you get a tally mark. Work until one partner gets seven tally marks.

**I can …**
add within 100.

**© Content Standard** 2.NBT.B.5
**Mathematical Practices** MP.3, MP.6, MP.7, MP.8

**Partner 1**

| 49 |
| 60 |
| 36 |
| 55 |
| 20 |

| 34 | 76 | 74 | 61 | 63 | 89 |
| 58 | 80 | 93 | 78 | 95 | 100 |
| 85 | 74 | 69 | 50 | 98 | 65 |
| 45 | 87 | 60 | 84 | 89 | 49 |

**Partner 2**

| 40 |
| 25 |
| 14 |
| 38 |
| 29 |

| **Tally Marks for Partner 1** | **Tally Marks for Partner 2** |

A-Z
Glossary

## Understand Vocabulary

Write *always*, *sometimes*, or *never*.

1. A bar diagram shows subtraction. _____

2. An 8 in the ones place of a number equals 80. _____

3. A 5 in the tens place of a number equals 50. _____

---

Draw a line from each term to its example.

4. equation

5. regroup

6. difference

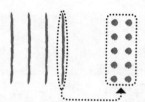

The answer to 75 − 23

72 + 25 = 97

---

## Use Vocabulary in Writing

7. Explain how you can make a model to show and help you solve the problem. Use terms from the Word List.

Molly has 64 marbles.
Leslie has 29 marbles.
How many fewer marbles does Leslie have?

**Set A**

You can use place-value blocks to find
46 – 8. You can regroup 1 ten as 10 ones
and then take away 8 ones.

| Tens | Ones |
|------|------|

46 – 8 = _38_

Did you need to regroup?

Yes          No

Subtract. You can use
place-value blocks to help.
Draw blocks to show
your work.

1. 61 – 3 = _____

| Tens | Ones |
|------|------|

2. 57 – 5 = _____

| Tens | Ones |
|------|------|

**Set B**

You can use place-value blocks to find 72 – 26.
First, take away the tens. Then regroup 1 ten as
10 ones and take away 6 ones.

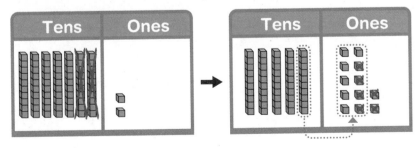

| Tens | Ones |
|------|------|

→

| Tens | Ones |
|------|------|

72 – 26 = _46_

Subtract. Use place-value blocks.
Show your work.

3. 27 – 11 = _____

| Tens | Ones |
|------|------|

4. 33 – 24 = _____

| Tens | Ones |
|------|------|

You can use place-value blocks and partial differences to find 53 − 37. First, subtract 3 tens from 5 tens. Then subtract 3 of the ones to make a 10. Then regroup 1 ten as 10 ones and subtract the other 4 ones.

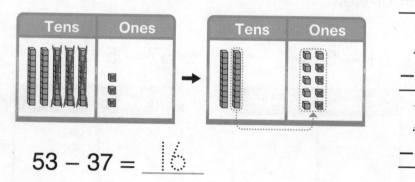

$$53 - 37 = \underline{16}$$

$$
\begin{array}{r}
53 \\
- 30 \\
\hline
23 \\
- 3 \\
\hline
20 \\
- 4 \\
\hline
16
\end{array}
$$

Subtract. Use place-value blocks to find partial differences. Record your work.

**5.** 22 − 14 = _____    **6.** 73 − 38 = _____

**7.** 45 − 25 = _____    **8.** 84 − 46 = _____

You can mentally break apart the number you are subtracting. Find 72 − 47.

Subtract 47 in parts. You can subtract the parts in any order and record partial differences.

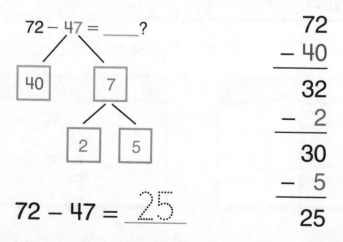

$$72 - 47 = \underline{25}$$

$$
\begin{array}{r}
72 \\
- 40 \\
\hline
32 \\
- 2 \\
\hline
30 \\
- 5 \\
\hline
25
\end{array}
$$

Subtract. Use partial differences. Break apart the number you are subtracting. Show your work.

**9.** 47 − 29 = _____    **10.** 55 − 36 = _____

**11.** 55 − 37 = _____    **12.** 77 − 53 = _____

Name _____

**Set E**

You can draw blocks, regroup, and record partial differences. Find 52 − 33. You can regroup 1 ten as 10 ones.

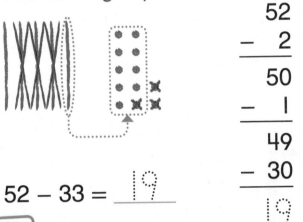

$$52$$
$$- \quad 2$$
$$\overline{50}$$
$$- \quad 1$$
$$\overline{49}$$
$$- 30$$
$$\overline{19}$$

52 − 33 = __19__

Use any strategy to subtract. Show your work.

13. 81 − 66 = _____   14. 96 − 19 = _____

15. 62 − 17 = _____   16. 57 − 29 = _____

**Set F**

48 people are at the beach. 16 people are swimming. The rest are playing volleyball. How many people are playing volleyball?

You can use a bar diagram and partial differences to solve the problem.

$$48$$
$$- \quad 6$$
$$\overline{42}$$
$$- 10$$
$$\overline{32}$$

__32__ people are playing volleyball.

Solve the problem. Show your work.

17. Mark has 33 stickers. 16 stickers are green. The rest are yellow. How many stickers are yellow?

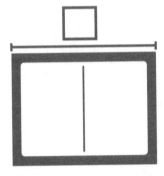

_____ yellow stickers

## Thinking Habits

Reasoning

What do the numbers and symbols in the problem mean?

How are the numbers in the problem related?

How can I show a word problem using pictures or numbers?

Complete the bar diagram and write an equation to show the problem. Then solve. Show your work.

18. 94 bricks are needed to build a wall. Lindy has 65 bricks. How many more bricks does she need?

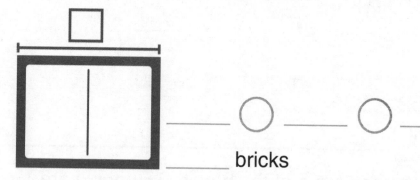

_____ bricks

19. Explain why making a bar diagram can help you solve the problem above.

_____

_____

_____

_____

_____

_____

**1.** Which is the difference of 55 − 7?
You may draw place-value blocks.

Ⓐ 45

Ⓑ 46

Ⓒ 47

Ⓓ 48

| Tens | Ones |
| --- | --- |
|  |  |

**2.** Sam has 74 books.
He puts 28 books on a shelf.
How many books are **NOT**
on the shelf? Show your work.

_____ books are **NOT** on the shelf.

**3.** A ship has 68 round windows.
The ship also has 16 square windows.
7 of the windows are broken. How many
windows are **NOT** broken?

Ⓐ 45

Ⓑ 61

Ⓒ 77

Ⓓ 91

**4.** Ryan has 46 marbles.
John has 4 fewer marbles than Ryan.
John gives 9 marbles to his friend.

**A.** Which pair of equations should be used
to find how many marbles John has now?

Ⓐ $46 - 4 = 42$
$42 - 9 = 33$

Ⓒ $46 + 4 = 50$
$50 - 9 = 41$

Ⓑ $46 - 4 = 42$
$42 + 9 = 51$

Ⓓ $46 + 4 = 50$
$50 + 9 = 59$

**B.** How many marbles does John have now?

_____

**5.** Jason wants to find 86 − 61 using place-value blocks.

Will Jason need to regroup to find the difference? Which is correct?

Ⓐ Yes; 86 should be regrouped as 8 tens and 16 ones.

Ⓑ Yes; 61 should be regrouped as 5 tens and 11 ones.

Ⓒ Yes; 86 should be regrouped as 7 tens and 16 ones.

Ⓓ No; Regrouping is not needed.

**6.** A book has 72 pages. Dan reads 38 pages on Monday. He reads 26 pages on Tuesday. How many pages does Dan have left to read?

**A.** Which pair of equations should be used to find how many pages Dan has left to read?

Ⓐ $38 + 26 = 64$
$72 - 64 = 8$

Ⓒ $72 + 26 = 98$
$98 - 38 = 60$

Ⓑ $72 - 38 = 34$
$34 + 26 = 60$

Ⓓ $72 - 26 = 46$
$46 + 38 = 84$

**B.** How many pages does Dan have left to read? _____

**7.** Circle the problem that you will use regrouping of place-value blocks to solve. Then draw blocks to show how you know.

$54 - 23$      $82 - 44$

**8.** Claire has 53 beads. Grace has 26 beads. Bella has 39 beads. How many fewer beads does Bella have than Claire?

Show how you can break apart a number and use partial differences to solve.

_____ fewer beads

9. Which numbers will complete this partial differences problem for 54 − 18? Choose all that apply.

$$\begin{array}{r} 54 \\ -\ 10 \\ \hline ? \\ -\ 4 \\ \hline 40 \\ -\ 4 \\ \hline ? \end{array}$$

☐ 34

☐ 36

☐ 44

☐ 45

☐ 53

10. Use any strategy to find 24 − 16. Show your work. Write the missing part in the bar diagram.

24 − 16 = _____

11. Peter collects 54 stamps. He gives 29 stamps to Ruth. How many stamps does Peter have now? Show the problem in the bar diagram with a ? for the unknown number. Then write an equation to solve the problem.

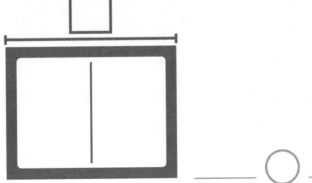

_____ ◯ _____ = _____ stamps

**12.** Find 53 – 27. Use partial differences to solve. Show your work.

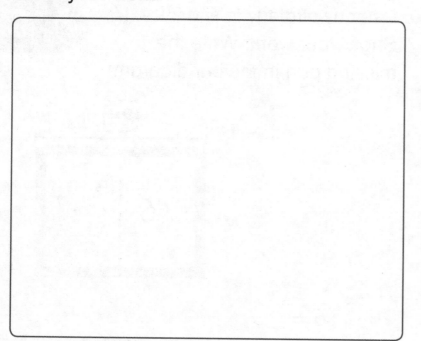

53 – 27 = _____

**13.** Choose all of the problems that you will solve by regrouping if you subtract using place-value blocks. Draw blocks if needed.

☐  45 – 0 = ?

☐  68 – 49 = ?

☐  84 – 37 = ?

☐  99 – 33 = ?

☐  78 – 18 = ?

**14.** Find 72 – 38.
Use any strategy to solve. Then explain why your strategy works.

**Topic 6** | Assessment Practic

**Stamp Collection**

Mary collects stamps.
The table shows the number of different kinds of stamps that she has.

Performance Task

| Number of Stamps ||
|------------|----|
| Flags | 8 |
| Butterflies | 34 |
| Birds | 27 |
| Flowers | 61 |

1. How many more stamps with butterflies does Mary have than stamps with flags? Choose a strategy to solve. Show your work.

_____ more stamps with butterflies

2. How many fewer stamps with birds does Mary have than stamps with flowers? Use a different strategy to solve. Show your work.

_____ fewer stamps with birds

3. Explain why the strategy you chose in Item 2 works.

_____
_____
_____
_____
_____

**4.** Luke also collects stamps.
He has 57 stamps.
His friend gives him 25 more stamps.

Then Luke gives away some stamps.
Now Luke has 44 stamps.
How many stamps did Luke give away?

### Part A

How many stamps does Luke have
after his friend gives him more stamps?

_____ ◯ _____ = _____

_____ stamps

### Part B

How many stamps did Luke give away?

_____ ◯ _____ = _____

_____ stamps

**5.** Mary puts 54 of her stamps in a book.
The book holds 96 stamps.
How many more stamps can Mary put in
the book?

### Part A

Complete the bar diagram to model the problem

Explain how the bar diagram helps you
understand the problem.

_____

_____

_____

_____

_____

### Part B

Write an equation to solve the problem.

_____ ◯ _____ = _____

_____ more stamps

# More Solving Problems Involving Addition and Subtraction

**Digital Resources**

Interactive Student Edition · Activity · Visual Learning · Video · Practice

Assessment · Games · Tools · Glossary

**Essential Question:** How can you solve word problems that use adding or subtracting?

This row of trees can help slow down the wind!

This is only one of the ways to help protect land from wind or water.

Wow! Let's do this project and learn more.

## ēnVision STEM Project: Solving Problems

**Find Out** Find and share books that tell about ways to protect land from damage that wind or water can cause. Compare the different ways to protect the land.

**Journal: Make a Book** Show what you learn in a book. In your book, also:

- Show ways to solve problems caused by wind or water.

- Show ways to solve problems using addition or subtraction.

Name _____

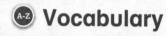

## Review What You Know

### Vocabulary

1. Write the subtraction problem below as an **equation**.

$$\begin{array}{r} 75 \\ -\ 30 \\ \hline 45 \end{array}$$

2. Complete the **bar diagram** to model $77 + 22 = ?$

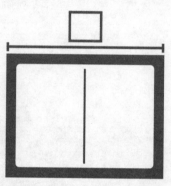

3. Circle the two addends below that are **compatible numbers**.

$$18 + 6 + 4 = ?$$

### Adding to Check Subtraction

4. Use addition to check if the subtraction equation is correct.

$$51 - 22 = 29$$

Is it correct? _____

### Subtracting to Check Addition

5. Use subtraction to check if the addition is correct.

$$37 + 26 = 53$$

Is it correct? _____

### Number Story

6. Jim and Maria are counting birds. Jim counts 17 birds. Maria counts 33 birds. How many more birds does Maria count than Jim?

_____ more birds

Name _____

**PROJECT 7A**

## How many points has your favorite hockey player scored?

**Project:** Design a Player Card

**PROJECT 7B**

## How many floors do New York City skyscrapers have?

**Project:** Build a Skyscraper Model

**PROJECT 7C**

## Where can you find caves in the United States?

**Project:** Create a Worksheet of Cave Problems

Video

## Math Modeling

## The Water Jug

Before watching the video, think:

Did you know that feeling hungry could actually mean you are thirsty? The best way to tell is to drink a glass of water and wait 15 minutes. If you are still hungry, it's time to eat!

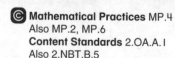

## I can ...

model with math to solve a problem that involves using strategies to add and subtract.

© **Mathematical Practices** MP.4
Also MP.2, MP.6
**Content Standards** 2.OA.A.1
Also 2.NBT.B.5

Name _____

Jenn has some red cubes and 11 blue cubes. She has 24 red and blue cubes in all.

She says the problem can be shown with the equation below.

$$? + 11 = 24$$

Draw what the ? represents.
Explain your answer.

**I can ...**
model problems using equations with unknowns in any position.

 **Content Standards** 2.OA.A.1
Also 2.NBT.B.5
**Mathematical Practices** MP.2, MP.4, MP.8

Robert has 27 toy robots. He buys some more. Now he has 58 robots. How many robots did Robert buy?

58 is the whole. 27 is one part.

You can show the problem with an equation.

$$27 + ? = 58$$

The ? shows the addend you don't know.

58

| 27 | ? |

You can solve the problem by adding on from 27 until you get to 58.

$27 + 10 = 37$
$37 + 10 = 47$
$47 + 10 = 57$
$57 + 1 = 58$

$10 + 10 + 10 + 1 = 31$
So, $27 + 31 = 58$.

Robert bought 31 robots.

You can subtract to solve the problem.

$58 - 27$

20        7

$58 - 20 = 38$
$38 - 7 = 31$

You can check by adding.
$31 + 27 = 58$

Robert bought 31 robots.

---

**Convince Me!** Could you show Robert's robot problem with the equation below? Explain.

$$58 = 27 + ?$$

**Guided Practice** Write an equation with a ? for the unknown to model the problem. Then solve. Show your work.

1. Mary has some game tickets. She gives away 14 tickets and now has 17 tickets left. How many tickets did she have at first?

Equation: $? - 14 = 17$ _____ tickets

2. Tamara has $25. She earns $34 more by working. How much money does she have now?

Equation: _____ $ _____

**Independent Practice**   Write an equation with a ? for the unknown to model the problem. Then solve. Show your work.

3. Erin has 32 books on her bookshelf. She gives some to friends and now has 19 books left. How many books did she give away?

   Equation: _____

   _____ books

4. A store sells 38 men's bikes and 47 women's bikes. How many bikes did the store sell in all?

   Equation: _____

   _____ bikes

5. enVision® STEM A field has 25 trees in it. 14 trees are new and the rest are old. How many trees are old? Write two different equations that represent the problem. Then solve.

   Equation: _____

   Equation: _____

   _____ old trees

6. **Number Sense** Harry buys 22 fish. He has a round fish bowl and a rectangular fish tank. How could he place the fish in the bowl and tank?

   Equation: _____

   _____ fish in the bowl _____ fish in the tank

7. **Model** Rodney collects 17 leaves and Sheila collects 23 leaves. How many more leaves does Sheila collect than Rodney?

Equation: _____

_____ more leaves

8. **Model** Jun swims 18 laps and Mara swims 25 laps. How many fewer laps did Jun swim than Mara?

Equation: _____

_____ fewer laps

9. **Higher Order Thinking** Jim has 44 roses. 14 are white and the rest are red. How many are red? Write two different equations to model the problem. Then solve.

Equation: _____

Equation: _____

_____ red roses

10. ☑ **Assessment Practice** Some wolves howl in the woods. 12 wolves join them. Now 30 wolves howl. How many wolves howled at first?

Which equation models the problem? Choose all that apply.

- ☐ $? + 12 = 30$
- ☐ $30 = 12 + ?$
- ☐ $30 + 12 = ?$
- ☐ $30 = ? + 12$

Name _____

Solve & Share

Aiden has 27 fewer crayons this week than last week. Last week he had 56 crayons. How many crayons does Aiden have this week? Show your work.

**I can ...**
use drawings and equations to make sense of the words in problems.

© **Content Standards** 2.OA.A.1
Also 2.NBT.B.5
**Mathematical Practices** MP.1,
MP.2, MP.4

_____ crayons

Sally has 28 fewer blocks than Nigel.
Sally has 26 blocks.
How many blocks does Nigel have?

Let's think about who has fewer blocks and who has more blocks.

A bar diagram can help you think about the problem.

Nigel's blocks

? 

26 | 28

Sally's blocks | 28 blocks fewer

26 + 28 = ?

Sally has 28 fewer blocks than Nigel. That means Nigel has more blocks than Sally. You need to add!

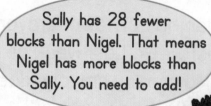

Nigel has 54 blocks.

**Convince Me!** How are these statements alike and different? Cal has 12 fewer blocks than Mia. Mia has 12 more blocks than Cal.

**Guided Practice** Solve the problem any way you choose. Use drawings and equations to help.

1. Lakota has 11 fewer magnets than Jeffrey. Lakota has 25 magnets. How many magnets does Jeffrey have?

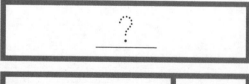

25 (+) 11 = ____

____ magnets

Tools   Assessment

**Independent Practice**   Solve each problem any way you choose. Use drawings and equations to help. Show your work.

2. There are 28 more students than adults at the school fair. There are 96 students at the school fair. How many adults are at the school fair?

_____ adults

3. Ellie the elephant has some peanuts. She eats 49 peanuts. Now Ellie the elephant has 31 peanuts. How many peanuts did she have before?

_____ peanuts

4. The blue team scores 16 fewer points than the green team. The blue team scores 41 points. How many points did the green team score?

_____ points

5. **Higher Order Thinking** Sean studies 16 fewer vocabulary words than Chris. Chris studies 10 fewer vocabulary words than Tia. Tia studies 34 words. How many words does Sean study? Explain your answer.

_____

_____

_____

**Problem Solving** Solve the problem any way you choose. Use drawings and equations to help. Show your work.

**6. Reasoning** Kevin practices kicks for soccer. He kicks 13 times at recess. He kicks 14 times after school. Then he kicks 16 times before bed. How many practice kicks did Kevin take in all?

I can think about what the numbers in the problem mean.

_____ kicks

**7. Higher Order Thinking** There are 48 red tacks and blue tacks in a bag. There are fewer red tacks than blue tacks. There are at least 26 blue tacks but no more than 30 blue tacks. How many of each color could be in the bag?

Complete the chart to solve the problem.

| Red Tacks | Blue Tacks | Total |
|-----------|-----------|-------|
| 22 | 26 | 48 |
| 21 | | 48 |
| | 28 | 48 |
| 19 | | 48 |
| | 30 | 48 |

**8.** ☑ **Assessment Practice** Jim has 14 fewer baseball cards than Sara. Sara has 27 cards. How many baseball cards does Jim have?

Draw a line to show where each number and the unknown could be in the equation. Then solve.

| 27 | ? | 14 |

_____ − _____ = _____

_____ cards

Name _____

Activity

# Lesson 7-3

## Continue Practice with Addition and Subtraction Problems

**Solve & Share**

Erin has 17 more books than Isabella. Erin has 44 books. How many books does Isabella have?

Solve any way you choose. Show your work.

### I can ...
use drawings and equations to make sense of the words in problems.

© **Content Standards** 2.OA.A.1 Also 2.NBT.B.5
**Mathematical Practices** MP.1, MP.2, MP.4

_____ **books**

Julie has 18 more pictures than Landon.
Julie has 37 pictures. How many pictures does Landon have?

Julie's pictures

| 37 |
|---|

| ? | 18 |
|---|---|

Landon's    18 pictures
pictures    more

The diagram helps you show what you know.

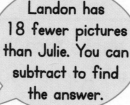

Landon has 18 fewer pictures than Julie. You can subtract to find the answer.

$37 - 18 = ?$

Since $18 = 17 + 1$, you can subtract 17 and then 1.

$37 - 17 = 20$

$20 - 1 = 19$

So, Landon has 19 pictures.

You can solve word problems using models, drawings, or mental math.

**Convince Me!** Compare the two statements:
Sam has 18 more markers than Zoey.
Zoey has 18 fewer markers than Sam.

☆ **Guided Practice** ☆  Solve the problem any way you choose. Use drawings and equations to help.

1. The second grade has 19 more students than the first grade. The second grade has 68 students. How many students does the first grade have?

| 68 |
|---|

| ? | 19 |
|---|---|

$68 \bigcirc 19 = \underline{\quad}$

_____ students

## Independent Practice

Solve each problem any way you choose. Use drawings and equations to help. Show your work.

**2.** There are 11 more adults than children at a craft fair. There are 54 adults at the craft fair. How many children are at the craft fair?

_____ children

**3.** Caleb is 17 years old. His sister is 12 years younger. How old is Caleb's sister?

_____ years old

**4.** Dylan and his friends had some blueberries. They ate 39 blueberries. They have 21 blueberries left. How many blueberries did Dylan and his friends have at first?

_____ blueberries

**5. enVision® STEM** Addison made a dam with 18 more rocks than James. Addison's dam had 42 rocks. How many rocks did James's dam have? Explain your answer.

_____

_____

_____

_____

Solve the problem any way you choose. Use drawings and equations to help. Show your work.

6. **Reasoning** Connor has 39 sheets of green paper and some sheets of yellow paper. He has 78 sheets of paper in all. How many yellow sheets of paper does Connor have?

> I can think about how the numbers in the problem are related.

 yellow sheets

7. **Higher Order Thinking** There are 58 red pens and blue pens in a bag. There are more red pens than blue pens. There are at least 36 red pens but no more than 40 red pens. How many of each color could be in the bag?

Complete the chart to solve the problem.

| Red Pens | Blue Pens | Total |
|----------|-----------|-------|
| 36 | 22 | 58 |
| 37 | | 58 |
| | 20 | 58 |
| 39 | | 58 |
| | 18 | 58 |

8. ☑ **Assessment Practice** Andrew has 63 more beanbags than Evan. Andrew has 92 beanbags. How many beanbags does Evan have?

The bar diagram models the problem. Which is the missing number?

| 92 |
|----|

| ? | 63 |
|---|----|

Ⓐ 19
Ⓑ 29
Ⓒ 31
Ⓓ 39

Name _____

**Solve & Share**

3 bees land on some flowers.
10 more bees join them. Then 4 bees fly away.
How many bees are left?

Solve the problem any way you choose.
Write equations to show how you solved each part
of the problem.

**I can ...**
model and solve two-step
problems using equations.

© **Content Standards** 2.OA.A.1
Also 2.NBT.B.5
**Mathematical Practices** MP.1,
MP.2, MP.4

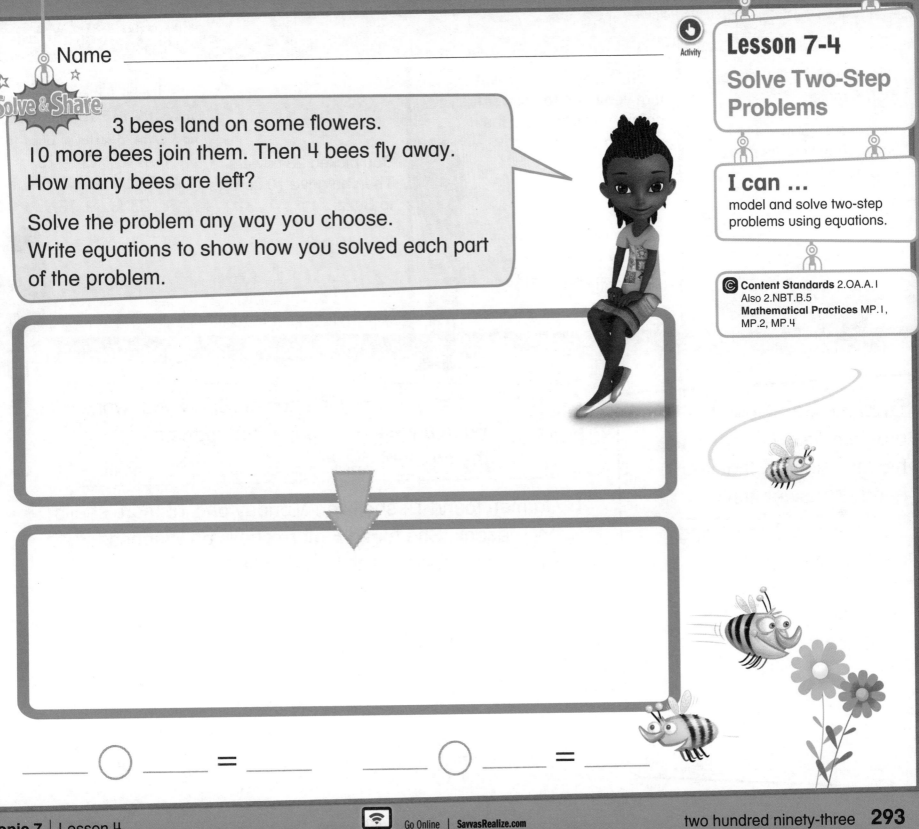

_____ ◯ _____ = _____    _____ ◯ _____ = _____

Bop picked 18 flowers and then 5 more.

He gave 10 flowers to Buzz. How many flowers does Bop have now?

Look for the hidden question that you need to answer first, before you can solve the problem.

The hidden question is "How many flowers did Bop pick in all?"

$18 + 5 = ?$

$\underline{18} + \underline{5} = \underline{23}$

Bop picked 23 flowers. Then he gave 10 flowers to Buzz.

$23 - 10 = ?$

$\underline{23} - \underline{10} = \underline{13}$

Now Bop has 13 flowers.

I added 2 ones to make the next ten and then added the 3 leftover ones to find $18 + 5 = 23$. Then I subtracted 10 from 23 to get 13.

**Convince Me!** Read the problem below. What is the hidden question that you need to answer first?

Tom buys 15 pencils and then 7 more. He gives 10 pencils to Nyla. How many pencils does Tom have now?

☆ **Guided Practice** ☆ Solve any way you choose. Show your work. Write equations to solve both parts of the problem.

1. Carmen found 14 shells on Monday and 15 more shells on Tuesday. She found 6 more shells on Wednesday. How many shells did she have then?

$\underline{14} \, \oplus \, \underline{15} = \underline{29}$

$\underline{29} \, \oplus \, \underline{6} = \underline{\phantom{00}}$

_____ shells

**Topic 7 | Lesson 4**

ame _____

 Tools    Assessment

## Independent Practice

Solve any way you choose. Show your work.
Write equations to solve both parts of the problem.

---

**2.** There are 6 red birds and 17 brown birds in a tree. If 8 more brown birds come, how birds will there be in all?

_____ ◯ _____ = _____

_____ ◯ _____ = _____

_____ birds

---

**3.** Erika saw 16 frogs on a lily pad and 8 frogs in the mud. If 7 of the frogs hop away, how many frogs will be left?

_____ ◯ _____ = _____

_____ ◯ _____ = _____

_____ frogs

> Think: How can I break apart the problem into steps? What is the hidden problem that I need to solve first?

---

**4. Higher Order Thinking** Kevin has 15 photos in his scrapbook. He adds 21 photos. Then Kevin takes out some photos. Now he has 28 photos in the scrapbook. How many photos did Kevin take out?

_____ ◯ _____ = _____

_____ ◯ _____ = _____

_____ photos

Topic 7 | Lesson 4

two hundred ninety-five **295**

5. **Model** There are 35 test questions.
Kareem answers 10 of the questions.
Then he answers 12 more questions.
How many more questions does
Kareem still need to answer?

_____ ◯ _____ = _____

_____ ◯ _____ = _____

_____ more questions

---

6. **(A-Z) Vocabulary** Circle the **equations**
that have a **sum**. Underline the equations
that have a **difference**.

$$33 - 18 = 15$$
$$79 + 16 = 95$$
$$46 + 34 = 80$$
$$52 - 52 = 0$$

7. **Algebra** Find the missing numbers.

$$35 + \blacksquare = 100 \qquad \blacksquare = \_\_\_$$

$$100 - \blacktriangle = 18 \qquad \blacktriangle = \_\_\_$$

---

8. **Higher Order Thinking** There are
25 friends at a party. Another 20 friends
arrive. Then some friends leave the party.
Only 7 friends stay. How many friends
leave the party?

Write two equations to solve the problem.

_____

_____ friends leave the party.

9. **☑ Assessment Practice** Bill caught 22 fish
and threw 6 fish back. He caught 8 more fish.
How many fish does Bill have now?

Which equations can be used to solve the
problem?

Ⓐ $22 + 6 = 28$ and $28 - 8 = 20$

Ⓑ $22 - 6 = 16$ and $8 - 6 = 2$

Ⓒ $22 - 6 = 16$ and $16 + 8 = 24$

Ⓓ $22 + 6 = 28$ and $28 + 8 = 36$

**Solve & Share**

You have 26 library books. You return some books. Then you take out 15 more books. Now you have 27 books. How many books did you return?

Solve any way you choose. Show your work.

**I can ...**
use different ways to solve two-step problems.

© **Content Standards** 2.OA.A.1
Also 2.NBT.B.5
**Mathematical Practices** MP.1, MP.3, MP.4

Mia sees 15 yellow birds and 16 red birds. Some birds fly away and now Mia sees 14 birds. How many birds flew away?

I need to solve the first step of the problem in order to solve the second step.

?

| 15 | 16 |

15 + 16 = ?
+5   −5
20 + 11 = 31

Mia sees ___31___ birds in all.

31

| ? | 14 |

31 − 14 = ?
      / \
    10   4
31 − 10 = 21
21 −  4 = 17

There are 14 birds left after ___17___ fly away.

Bar diagrams help me model the parts and the whole.

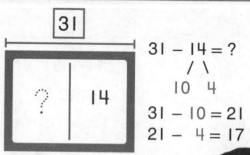

**Convince Me!** Why do you need two steps to solve the problem above?

☆ **Guided Practice**  Complete the equations to solve.

1. There are some boys painting and 9 girls painting. In all, 17 children are painting. Then some more boys come to paint. Now there are 15 boys painting. How many more boys come to paint?

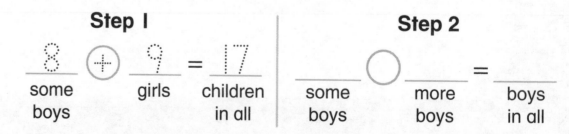

**Step 1**

__8__ (+) __9__ = __17__

some boys · girls · children in all

**Step 2**

___ ◯ ___ = ___

some boys · more boys · boys in all

_____ more boys come to paint.

**Topic 7** | Lesson

**Independent Practice**   Solve each problem any way you choose. Show your work.

2. Jake has 16 toy cars. Lidia has 5 fewer toy cars than Jake. How many toy cars do they have in all?

They have _____ cars in all.

3. Sandy has 12 balloons. Tom has 11 more balloons than Sandy. Some of Tom's balloons popped and now he has 14 balloons. How many balloons popped?

_____ balloons popped.

4. 25 wolves howl together in the woods. 14 wolves join them. Then 22 wolves run away. How many wolves are left?

_____ wolves are left.

5. **Higher Order Thinking** Explain how you solved Item 4.

_____

_____

_____

_____

6. **Make Sense** Tim bakes 24 more muffins than Gina. Gina bakes 13 muffins. Lea bakes 16 fewer muffins than Tim.

How many muffins does Lea bake?

I can check that my work and answer make sense.

_____ muffins

7. **Higher Order Thinking** Write a two-step number story using the numbers 36, 65, and 16. Then solve the problem. Write equations to show each step.

_____

_____

_____

_____

____ ◯ ____ = ____

____ ◯ ____ = ____

8. ☑ **Assessment Practice**
There are 44 marbles in a jar. Some are red and 23 are blue. Julie adds 13 red marbles to the jar. How many red marbles are in the jar now?

Which equations show a way to solve the problem?

Ⓐ 44 − 23 = 21
   21 + 13 = 34

Ⓒ 23 + 21 = 44
   44 − 13 = 31

Ⓑ 44 − 23 = 21
   21 − 13 = 8

Ⓓ 23 + 44 = 67
   67 + 13 = 80

Name _____

**Solve & Share**

What number goes in the blank to make this equation true? Show how you found out.

**I can ...**
fill in missing numbers in equations to make them true.

© **Content Standards** 2.NBT.B
Also 2.OA.B.2
**Mathematical Practices** MP.2, MP.3, MP.6

$$17 - 9 = 6 + \underline{\hspace{1cm}}$$

Find the missing number to make the equation true.

$18 + 10 = 34 - ?$

"=" means the value on both sides is the same. I can find $18 + 10$ first.

$18 + 10 = 28$

---

$28 = 34 - ?$

$18 + 10 = 28.$
So, 28 equals 34 minus some number.

---

What number can you subtract from 34 to get 28?

$28 = 34 - ?$

I can count on by ones from 28 to 34. I counted on 6.

$28 + 2 = 30$
$30 + 4 = 34$

So, $28 = 34 - 6.$

---

The missing number is 6.

$18 + 10 = 34 - 6$
$28 = 28$ ✔

Make sure both sides of the equal sign have the same value.

So, $18 + 10 = 34 - \underline{6}$.

---

**Convince Me!** What number goes in the blank to make this equation true? Explain how you know.

$\underline{\phantom{000}} - 5 = 14 - 7$

---

☆ **Guided Practice** ☆ Write the missing numbers to make the equations true.

1.      $15 - ? = 2 + 4$

         $15 - ? = \underline{6}$

     $15 - \underline{9} = 6$

     So,

     $15 - \underline{9} = 2 + 4.$

2. $25 + 10 = 43 - ?$

     $\underline{\phantom{000}} = 43 - ?$

     $\underline{\phantom{000}} = 43 - \underline{\phantom{000}}$

     So,

     $25 + 10 = 43 - \underline{\phantom{000}}.$

---

**Independent Practice**  Write the missing number that makes each equation true. Show your work.

3. $9 + \underline{\hspace{1cm}} = 8 + 8$

4. $16 - 8 = 10 - \underline{\hspace{1cm}}$

5. $\underline{\hspace{1cm}} - 4 = 16 - 5$

6. $17 - 12 = 10 - \underline{\hspace{1cm}}$

7. $\underline{\hspace{1cm}} - 3 = 5 + 12$

8. $18 - \underline{\hspace{1cm}} = 3 + 6$

9. $27 + 20 = 17 + \underline{\hspace{1cm}}$

10. $56 - 20 = 30 + \underline{\hspace{1cm}}$

11. $45 - 10 = 40 - \underline{\hspace{1cm}}$

12. **Algebra** Write the missing number in the equation below. Explain how you know.

$\underline{\hspace{1cm}} + 5 + 6 = 6 + 9 + 5$

I can solve the problem without adding!

13. **Reasoning** Teresa has 4 daisies and 5 roses. Sam has 15 flowers. How many flowers would Sam need to give away so that he has the same number of flowers as Teresa?

_____ flowers

14. **Reasoning** Karen had $14 and spent $6. Larry had some money and spent $3. Now Karen and Larry have the same amount of money. How much money did Larry have before he spent $3?

$_____

15. **Higher Order Thinking** Todd has the same number of fruits and vegetables. He has 3 apples and 7 oranges. He has 6 carrots and some onions. How many onions does Todd have? Tell how you know.

_____

_____

_____

_____

16. ☑ **Assessment Practice** Match each number with the equation it is missing from.

$1 + 3 = 12 -$ _____          6

_____ $+ 2 = 6 + 6$          10

$4 + 7 = 5 +$ _____          8

_____ $- 2 = 12 - 7$          7

Name _____

Solve & Share

Find the missing number to make the equation true. Show your work.

$$? - 9 = 22 - 7$$

How could you check your work? Is there a tool you could use? Explain.

## Lesson 7-7
## Continue to Make True Equations

### I can ...
find the missing number in equations to make equations true.

**Content Standard** 2.NBT.B
**Mathematical Practices** MP.2, MP.3, MP.5

_____ $- 9 = 22 - 7$

Find the missing number to make this equation true.

$45 + 10 + 10 = ? + 19$

I will solve $45 + 10 + 10$ first.

$45 + 10 = 55$
$55 + 10 = 65$

$65 = ? + 19$

The equal sign means "the same value as." 65 has the same value as some number added to 19.

What number can you add to 19 to get 65?

I can count on from 19 by 10s and 1s until I reach 65.

19, 29, 39, 49, 59, 60, 61, 62, 63, 64, 65.

I counted on 4 tens and 6 ones. So, I counted on 46.

The missing number is 46.

$65 = 46 + 19$

I can check my work.

$46 + 19$
$-1 \quad +1$
$45 + 20 = 65$

So,
$45 + 10 + 10 = \underline{46} + 19$

---

**Convince Me!** What number goes in the blank to make this equation true? Explain how you know.

$33 + 10 + 7 = \underline{\phantom{000}} + 25$

**Guided Practice** Write the missing numbers to make the equations true.

1. $8 + 10 + 12 = ? + 20$

$8 + 10 + 12 = \underline{30}$

$30 = \underline{10} + 20$

So,

$8 + 10 + 12 = \underline{10} + 20$

2. $20 + 13 + 7 = 49 - ?$

$20 + 13 + 7 = \underline{\phantom{00}}$

$40 = 49 - \underline{\phantom{00}}$

So,

$20 + 13 + 7 = 49 - \underline{\phantom{00}}$

**Topic 7** | Lesson

Tools  Assessment

**ndependent Practice** Find the missing number that makes each equation true. Show your work.

**3.** $25 + \underline{\quad} = 6 + 20 + 4$

**4.** $10 + 3 + 27 = 30 + \underline{\quad}$

**5.** $48 - \underline{\quad} = 12 + 12 + 4$

**6.** $47 - 5 = 10 + 10 + \underline{\quad}$

**7.** $32 + 14 + 18 = 50 + \underline{\quad}$

**8.** $43 + 10 + 20 = 95 - \underline{\quad}$

**9.** $28 + 30 = 17 + 13 + \underline{\quad}$

**10.** $56 - 20 = 18 + 12 + \underline{\quad}$

**11.** $21 + 5 + 19 = 65 - \underline{\quad}$

**12. Algebra** Write the missing number in the equation. Explain how you know.

$\underline{\quad} + 25 + 18 = 18 + 20 + 25$

I can solve the problem without adding.

Write an equation to show each problem. Then solve. Show your work.

13. **Reasoning** Gemma had some game tokens and then earned 8 more. Ana had 32 tokens and lost 4. Now they have an equal number of tokens. How many tokens did Gemma have to start?

_____ tokens

14. **Reasoning** Jill and Tim have the same number of toy cars. Tim has 10 red cars and 20 blue cars. Jill has 8 red cars, 15 blue cars, and some yellow cars. How many yellow cars does Jill have?

_____ yellow cars

15. **Higher Order Thinking** Kate plays a card game with two friends. She gives 5 cards to each player. Ten plus what number is equal to the total number of cards Kate gives out?

Write an equation to show and solve the problem.

16. ☑ **Assessment Practice** Match each number with the equation it is missing from.

$8 + 17 + 5 = 49 - \underline{\quad}$      32

$\underline{\quad} + 12 = 6 + 6 + 20$      19

$8 + 20 + 12 = \underline{\quad} + 8$      20

$\underline{\quad} + 15 = 17 + 10 + 10$      22

Name _____

**Solve & Share**

Write a number story that has an answer of 20.

Then write an equation to match your story.

**I can ...**
use reasoning to write and solve number stories.

 **Mathematical Practices** MP.2
Also MP.1, MP.3, MP.4, MP.7
**Content Standards** 2.OA.A.1
Also 2.NBT.B.9

**Thinking Habits**

How are the numbers in the problem related?

How can I use a word problem to show what the equation means?

My equation:

Write a number story for 68 − 33. Then write an equation to match your story.

How can I show what numbers and symbols mean?

I think about what 68, 33 and the − sign mean in the problem. I can use that to write a story.

Subtraction stories can be about separating or about comparing. This story is about separating.

Harry finds 68 acorns. He gives 33 acorns to Joyce. How many acorns does Harry have left?

$$68 − 33 = ?$$

Subtract to answer the question in the problem.

68 − 33 = 35 So, Harry has 35 acorns left.

$$68 − 33 = ?$$
$$−3 \quad −3$$
$$65 − 30 = 35$$

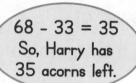

---

**Convince Me!** Write a number story about comparing for 68 − 33 = ?.

☆ **Guided Practice** ☆ Complete the number story. Then complete the equation to match the story. Draw a picture to help, if needed.

1. $47 − 18 =$ _____

Blake collects __47__ cans.

He recycles __18__ cans.

How many cans does Blake have now?

_____ cans

## Independent Practice

Write a number story to show the problem.
Complete the equation to match your story.

**2.** $22 - 17 =$ _____

_____

_____

_____

_____

**3.** $84 - 62 =$ _____

_____

_____

_____

_____

**4.** $28 + 12 =$ _____

_____

_____

_____

_____

**5.** $39 + 47 =$ _____

_____

_____

_____

_____

☑ **Performance Task**

**Toy Car Collection**
The picture at the right shows a toy car collection. Use the picture to write and solve number story problems.

**6. Reasoning** Write an addition story about the toy car collection.

_____

_____

_____

**7. Reasoning** Write a subtraction comparison story about the collection.

_____

_____

_____

**8. Model** Write an equation for each number story that you wrote in Item 6 and Item 7. Then solve any way you choose. Show your work.

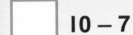

Find a partner. Point to a clue. Read the clue.

Look below the clues to find a match. Write the clue letter in the box next to the match.

Find a match for every clue.

**I can ...**
add and subtract within 20.

© **Content Standard** 2.OA.B.2
**Mathematical Practices** MP.3, MP.6, MP.7, MP.8

**Clues**

**A** Is equal to 5 + 4

**B** Is equal to 8 + 7

**C** Is equal to 20 – 10

**D** Is equal to 12 – 7

**E** Is equal to 9 + 3

**F** Is equal to 13 – 9

**G** Is equal to 11 – 8

**H** Is equal to 7 + 6

**I** Is equal to 2 + 4

**J** Is equal to 5 + 6

**K** Is equal to 14 – 7

**L** Is equal to 10 + 6

| ☐ 10 – 7 | ☐ 19 – 9 | ☐ 8 + 8 | ☐ 12 – 8 |
| ☐ 18 – 9 | ☐ 13 – 8 | ☐ 13 – 7 | ☐ 8 + 3 |
| ☐ 4 + 9 | ☐ 15 – 8 | ☐ 9 + 6 | ☐ 6 + 6 |

A-Z
Glossary

**Word List**
- bar diagram
- compatible numbers
- difference
- equation
- open number line
- regroup
- sum

## Understand Vocabulary

Write T for *true* or F for *false*.

1. _____ An equation is a model you can use to help solve a problem.

2. _____ 43 is the difference in the equation $43 - 16 = 27$.

3. _____ Addition and subtraction can be shown using a bar diagram.

4. _____ An equation is a model you can use to represent a problem.

5. _____ A sum is the answer to a subtraction problem.

Draw a line from each term to its example.

6. regroup

7. sum

8. open number line

The answer to $18 + 45$

15 ones = 1 ten and 5 ones

## Use Vocabulary in Writing

9. Explain how you can count on to find $58 + 23$. Use at least one term from the Word List.

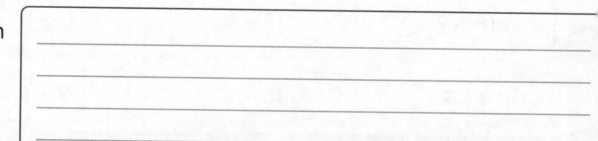

Name _____

**Set A**

You can model problems.

A store has some rings. Then 34 rings are sold. Now the store has 47 rings. How many rings did the store have at first?

$? - 34 = 47$

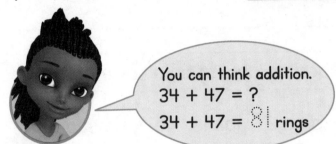

You can think addition.
$34 + 47 = ?$
$34 + 47 = 81$ rings

Write an equation with a ? for the unknown to represent the problem. Then solve using the bar diagram.

1. A store has 52 juice boxes. Then some juice boxes are sold. Now the store has 35 juice boxes. How many juice boxes were sold?

Equation: _____

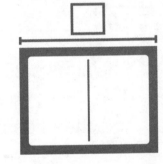

_____ juice boxes

**Set B**

Will has 19 fewer crayons than Kari. Kari has 25 crayons. How many crayons does Will have?

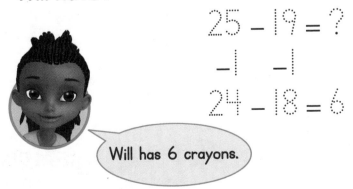

$25 - 19 = ?$
$-1 \quad -1$
$24 - 18 = 6$

Will has 6 crayons.

Solve the problem any way you choose. Show your work.

2. A building kit has 26 fewer green blocks than blue blocks. The kit has 44 green blocks. How many blue blocks are there?

_____ blue blocks

Trent has 29 more toy cars than Bill. Trent has 72 toy cars. How many toy cars does Bill have?

$$72 - 29 = ?$$

$$+ 1 \quad + 1$$

$$73 - 30 = 43$$

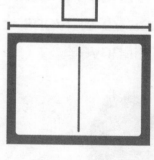

This means Bill has 29 fewer toy cars than Trent. Subtract to solve. Bill has 43 toy cars.

___43___ cars

Solve the problem any way you choose. Show your work.

3. A game has 19 more red cards than blue cards. The game has 43 red cards. How many blue cards does the game have?

_____ blue cards

Lacie buys 28 peaches. She gives 12 to Ted. Then she buys 15 more. How many peaches does Lacie have now?

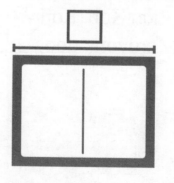

$$28 - 12 = \underline{16}$$

$$16 + 15 = \underline{31}$$

___31___ peaches

Use the bar diagrams to help solve both steps.

4. Craig scores 27 points. Next, he scores 33 points. Then he loses 14 points. How many points does Craig have now?

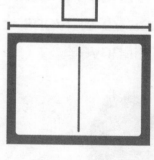

$$27 + 33 = \underline{\phantom{00}}$$

$$\underline{\phantom{00}} - \underline{\phantom{00}} = \underline{\phantom{00}}$$

_____ points

**Set E**

Jess had 16 white eggs and 13 brown eggs. She broke some eggs and was left with 18 eggs to sell. How many eggs did she break?

Solve the problem any way you choose. Show your work.

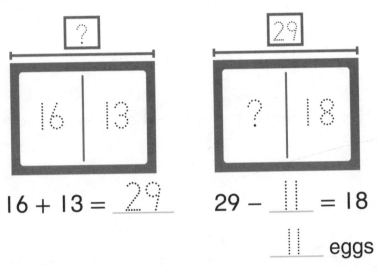

$16 + 13 = \underline{29}$       $29 - \underline{11} = 18$

$\underline{11}$ eggs

5. There are 36 raspberries and 24 blueberries in the fruit salad. Ben eats some. Now there are 45 berries left. How many berries did Ben eat?

_____ berries

**Set F**

Write the missing number to make the equation true.

$14 + 6 = \underline{\hspace{1cm}} + 12$

Both sides are equal.

$14 + 6 = 20$

So, $20 = \underline{8} + 12$.

The missing number is 8.

Find and write the missing numbers to make the equations true.

6. $4 + 8 = 19 - \underline{\hspace{0.5cm}}$

7. $\underline{\hspace{0.5cm}} + 7 = 12 + 2$

8. $15 + \underline{\hspace{0.5cm}} = 10 + 8$

9. $\underline{\hspace{0.5cm}} - 6 = 9 + 5$

10. $8 + 5 = \underline{\hspace{0.5cm}} - 3$

Find the missing number to make the equation true.

$7 + 8 + \underline{\phantom{00}} = 30 - 5$

First, you can find the value of the side with no missing number.

$$30 - 5 = 25$$

The two sides are equal. So,

$7 + 8 + \underline{\phantom{00}} = 25$

$15 + \underline{10} = 25$

$7 + 8 + \underline{10} = 30 - 5.$

The missing number is 10.

Find and write the missing numbers to make the equations true.

11. $13 + 7 + \underline{\phantom{00}} = 27 + 8$

12. $10 + 8 + 12 = 33 - \underline{\phantom{00}}$

13. $\underline{\phantom{00}} + 15 + 15 = 10 + 32$

14. $4 + 13 + 10 = \underline{\phantom{00}} - 13$

**Thinking Habits**

Reasoning

How are the numbers in the problem related?

How can I use a word problem to show what the equation means?

Write a number story for the problem. Complete the equation to match your story.

15. $28 + 35 = \underline{\phantom{0000}}$

_____

_____

_____

_____

**318** three hundred eighteen

1. Jodi has 28 apples. She buys some more. Now Jodi has 43 apples.
   How many apples did she buy?

   Use the bar diagram to help you write an equation.
   Then use the open number line to solve.

   _____ ◯ _____ = _____

   _____ apples

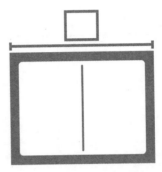

⟵——————————————————⟶

---

2. Alayna draws 18 more stars than Pearl. Alayna draws 37 stars.
   How many stars does Pearl draw?

   **A.** Can you use the equation to solve the problem? Choose Yes or No.

   $37 - 18 = ?$      ◯ Yes ◯ No

   $18 + 37 = ?$      ◯ Yes ◯ No

   $18 + ? = 37$      ◯ Yes ◯ No

   $? + 18 = 37$      ◯ Yes ◯ No

   **B.** How many stars does Pearl draw? _____ stars

3. Emily has 17 fewer ribbons than Piper. Piper has 48 ribbons. How many ribbons does Emily have?

Solve any way you choose. Show your work.

_____ ribbons

4. Write a number story for $72 - 36 = ?$. Then solve the story problem.

_____

_____

_____

$72 - 36 =$ _____

**Topic 7** | Assessment Practice

**5.** Joy needs 99 coats for children in need. She gets 54 coats from her school. She gets 22 coats from friends. How many more coats does Joy need?

Write equations to solve. Then write the answer.

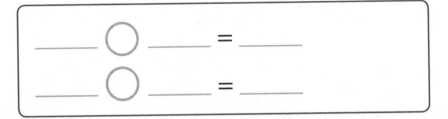

Joy needs _____ more coats.

---

**6.** Shane has 27 more cards than Tom. Shane has 62 cards. How many cards does Tom have?

Explain how you will solve the problem. Then solve.

Tom has _____ cards.

**7.** Grace collects cans to be recycled. The table shows the number of cans she has collected.

| Number of Cans | |
|---|---|
| Thursday | 12 |
| Friday | 29 |
| Saturday | 37 |

**A.** How many fewer cans did Grace collect on Thursday than on Saturday?

_____ fewer cans

**B.** Grace collects some more cans on Sunday. She now has 90 cans.

Find the missing number in the equation to find how many cans Grace collects on Sunday.

$12 + 29 + 37 +$ _____ $= 90$

**8.** Find the missing number that makes each equation true.

$18 - 10 = 9 -$ _____

$35 + 30 = 45 +$ _____

**9.** Find the missing number that makes each equation true.

$24 +$ _____ $= 7 + 15 + 8$

$46 - 5 = 10 + 10 +$ _____

Name _____

## School Fair

Meadow School is having a school fair. The table shows the number of tickets Ms. Davis's class has sold.

| Number of Tickets Sold | |
|---|---|
| Monday | 42 |
| Tuesday | 17 |
| Wednesday | 21 |

**1.** How many fewer tickets did Ms. Davis's class sell on Wednesday than on Monday?

Complete the bar diagram to model the problem. Then solve.

_____ fewer tickets

**2.** Ms. Davis says the class can have a party if they sell 95 tickets.

### Part A

Write an equation to show how many tickets the class has sold.

Then solve the equation. Show your work.

_____ tickets sold

### Part B

How many more tickets does the class have to sell to have a party? Explain.

_____ tickets

**3.** The table shows the number of tickets Mr. Rios's class has sold.

How many more tickets did his class sell in all on Monday and Tuesday than on Wednesday?

| Number of Tickets Sold | |
|---|---|
| Monday | 24 |
| Tuesday | 18 |
| Wednesday | 28 |

Write two equations to solve both parts of the problem.

_____ ◯ _____ = _____

_____ ◯ _____ = _____

_____ more tickets

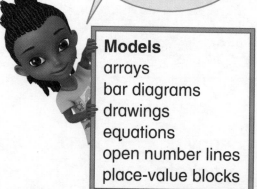

Here are some models you can use or make.

**Models**
arrays
bar diagrams
drawings
equations
open number lines
place-value blocks

**4. Part A**

Write a number story about selling tickets for the school fair. Use numbers that you can add or subtract.

_____

_____

_____

**Part B**

Write an equation to match your story. Then solve any way you choose. Show your work.

# Work with Time and Money

**Essential Question:** How can you solve problems about counting money or telling time to the nearest 5 minutes?

**Digital Resources**

Interactive Student Edition | Activity | Visual Learning | Video | Practice

Assessment | Games | Tools | Glossary

Different materials are used to make money!

How would you describe different types of money?

Wow! Let's do this project and learn more.

# ēnVision STEM Project: Money Matters

**Find Out** Collect examples of different types of coins and dollar bills. Describe how different coins and bills look and feel. Sort the money by size, color, and whether or not you can bend it.

**Journal: Make a Book** Show what you find out in a book. In your book, also:

- Tell how different types of coins are alike. Tell how they are different.

- Show as many different ways as you can to make 25¢.

Name _____

---

**A-Z Vocabulary**

1. Draw the hands to show **8 o'clock**.

2. Circle the number of minutes in one **hour**.

   30 minutes

   50 minutes

   60 minutes

3. Write the time below to the **half hour**.

   _____

---

**Doubles Facts**

4. Write each sum.

   $7 + 7 =$ _____

   $9 + 9 =$ _____

   $10 + 10 =$ _____

Doubles facts are fun.

**Array**

5. Use mental math. How many squares are in the array?

_____ squares

**Math Story**

6. Some pennies are in a cup. Jan takes out 22 of the pennies.
Now, 14 pennies are left in the cup. How many pennies were in the cup at the start?

_____ pennies

---

**326** three hundred twenty-six

Topic 8

**PROJECT 8A**

## What does a train schedule show?

**Project:** Make a Train Schedule Poster

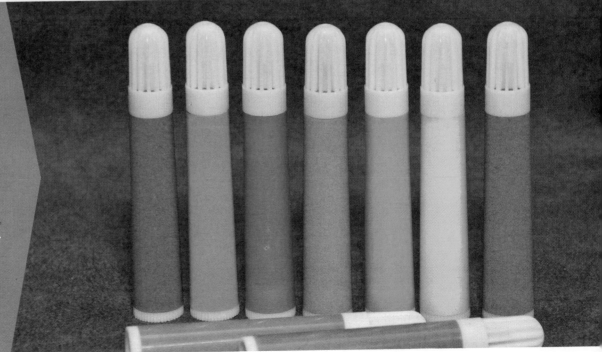

**North Concourse Departures**

| Time | Train Line | Destination | Track | Status |
|------|-----------|-------------|-------|--------|
| 1:35P | MILW-N | GRAYSLAKE | N5 | BOARDING |
| 1:40P | MILW-W | BIG TIMBER | N11 | ON TIME |
| 2:30P | MILW-W | BIG TIMBER | N15 | ON TIME |
| 2:35P | MILW-N | FOX LAKE | N9 | ON TIME |
| 3:35P | MILW-W | BIG TIMBER | N9 | ON TIME |
| 3:40P | MILW-N | FOX LAKE | N5 | ON TIME |
| 4:10P | MILW-W | FRANKLIN PARK | N9 | ON TIME |
| 4:16P | MILW-N | DEERFIELD | N5 | ON TIME |
| 4:25P | MILW-W | BIG TIMBER | N11 | ON TIME |
| 4:30P | N CENTRAL | ANTIOCH | N15 | ON TIME |
| 4:34P | MILW-W | FRANKLIN PARK | N13 | ON TIME |

**PROJECT 8B**

## How much do things cost?

**Project:** Create an Advertisement

Do you have the same schedule every day?

**Project:** Write a Daily Journal

What would you sell if you ran your own store?

**Project:** Set Up a Store

Activity

Solve & Share

Kelsey had 10 cents in her piggybank.
She finds 5 cents more and puts it in her bank.
Then Kelsey's mother gives her 20 cents to put in her bank.

How many cents does Kelsey have in her bank now?

**I can …**
solve problems with coins.

**Content Standards** 2.MD.C.8
Also 2.NBT.A.2
**Mathematical Practices** MP.1,
MP.2, MP.3

+5

10    15

+5      +10       +5

15  20      30  35

___35___ cents

 dime 10¢

nickel 5¢

penny 1¢

 quarter 25¢

 half-dollar 50¢

Micah has the coins shown below.
How many cents does Micah have?
Start with the coin of the **greatest value**.
Count on to the coin of the **least value**
to find the total value.

Micah has 91 cents.
The cent sign is ¢.

50¢   75¢   85¢   90¢   91¢

---

**Convince Me!** How many quarters have the same value as a half-dollar?

2Q = 1HD

How many dimes have the same value as a half-dollar?

5D = 1HD

How many cents would Micah have if he didn't have the half-dollar?

41

☆ **Guided Practice** Count on to find each total value.

1. Li has these coins. How many cents does Li have?

 → 31¢

10¢   20¢   25¢   30¢   31¢   Total

2. Manny has these coins. How many cents does Manny have?

 → 86¢

50¢   75¢ 85¢   86¢   Total

**Topic 8** | Lesson 1

**Solve & Share**

Grace has 40 cents. She gives Barry 24 cents. What coins could Grace have to start? How many cents does Grace have left? Explain.

**I can ...**
solve problems with coins.

Content Standards 2.MD.C.8
Also 2.NBT.A.2
Mathematical Practices MP.3, MP.4, MP.6

3   40
   − 24
   ─────
     16

16

Toby buys a toy dinosaur for 68¢.
He pays with 3 quarters.
How much change should Toby get?

68¢

First find out how much money Toby pays with.

25¢   50¢   75¢

Toby pays 75¢.

Then subtract the cost of the toy dinosaur from the amount Toby pays with.

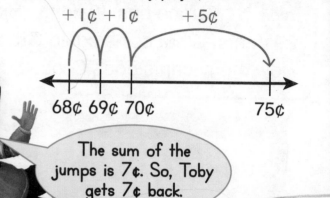

$+1¢ +1¢$        $+5¢$

68¢ 69¢ 70¢        75¢

The sum of the jumps is 7¢. So, Toby gets 7¢ back.

$75¢ - 68¢ = 7¢$

---

**Convince Me!** Why is subtracting 75¢ – 68¢ like subtracting 75 – 68? Explain.

☆ **Guided Practice** ☆   Solve each problem. Show your work.

1. Dora had some money in her pocket. She went to the mall and spent 3 dimes. Now Dora has 34¢. How much money was in her pocket before she went to the mall?

___?___ ¢ – __30__ ¢ = __34__ ¢

__30__ ¢ + __34__ ¢ = __64__ ¢

__64__ ¢

2. Peter has 58¢. His brother gave him 2 nickels and 3 pennies. How much money does Peter have now?

$58 + 13 = 71$

__70__ ¢

**Topic 8 | Lesson**

## Independent Practice ☆ Solve each problem. Show your work.

**3.** Marco buys an apple for 42¢. He pays with 4 dimes and 1 nickel. How much change should Marco get?

**4.** Trina buys a ring. She pays for it with 9 dimes. She receives 8 pennies in change. How much does the ring cost?

82

**5.** How many dimes have the same value as 2 quarters?

___5___ dimes

a half-dollar? ___5___ dimes

a dollar? ___10___ dimes

**6.** How many pennies have the same value as

a nickel? ___5¢___ pennies

a dime? ___10¢___ pennies

a quarter? ___25¢___ pennies

a dollar? ___100¢___ pennies

**7.** **Number Sense** What 5 coins have a total value of a quarter? Draw the coins. Label the value of each coin.

8. **enVision® STEM** Greg's science class wants to sort these coins by their color. What is the total value of the silver coins?

77 ¢

9. **Model** Rodney buys a banana for 43¢ and an orange for 37¢. Draw the fewest number of coins to show how Rodney could pay for the fruit.

10. **Higher Order Thinking** Ella has 4 dimes and 15 pennies. Marie has 3 quarters. Ella says she has more money because she has more coins. Is Ella correct? Explain.

11. ☑ **Assessment Practice** Lydia buys a toy car for 59¢. She pays with 6 dimes. Which shows how much change Lydia should get?

Ⓐ    Ⓒ

Ⓑ    Ⓓ

Name _____

Solve & Share

What is one way you can show 100¢ with coins? Use coins to model. Draw and label the coins you use.

I can ...
solve problems with money.

Content Standards 2.MD.C.8
Also 2.NBT.A.2
Mathematical Practices MP.2, MP.4, MP.7

100¢

Visual Learning · A-Z Glossary

This is **1 dollar**.
The **dollar sign** is **$**.

$1 bill
$1 = 100¢

Here are some other **dollar bills**.

$5 bill
$10 bill
$20 bill
$100 bill

Maria had these dollar bills. What is the total value?

$20  $30  $40  $45  $50  $51

20 + 10 + 10 + 5 + 5 + 1

Count on from the greatest bill to the least bill. Maria has $51.

---

**Convince Me!** How is counting dollar bills like counting coins? How is it different?

☆ **Guided Practice** Solve each problem.

1. Mr. Park has these dollar bills. Count on to find the total value.

$50.00

2. Ms. Lenz has these dollar bills. Count on to find the total value.

$36.00

Remember to count from the greatest bill to the least bill.

**Topic 8** | Lesson 3

**Solve & Share**

Billy, Sarah, and Maria have the same amount of money. Billy has a $1 bill. Sarah has only dimes. Maria has only nickels.

How many dimes does Sarah have?
How many nickels does Maria have?

Explain how you found your answers.

**I can ...**
solve problems about money.

© **Content Standards** 2.MD.C.8
Also 2.OA.A.1
**Mathematical Practices** MP.1,
MP.3, MP.6

$$\$1.00 = 100¢$$

$1 is the same as 100¢.

Sarah has ___10___ dimes.

Maria has ___20___ nickels.

Tammy has a $100 bill. She buys the game and the toy dog. How much money does she have left?

$25

$21

First add the cost of the game and the toy dog.

Game:          $25
Toy dog:    + $21
_____
Tens: $40
Ones:  $6
_____
Sum: $46

The game and the toy dog cost $46 in all.

Then add up to subtract the total cost of the game and the toy dog from $100.

+$10   +$10   +$10   +$10   +$10  +$4

$46    $56    $66    $76    $86    $96  $100

The sum of the jumps is $54. So, Tammy has $54 left.

$100 − $46 = $54

---

**Convince Me!** Tina solves the problem above by subtracting $100 − $25 and then subtracting $21 from that difference. Do you think she got the same answer as Tammy? Explain.

☆ **Guided Practice** ☆  Solve each problem. Show your work.

1. Sam had some money in his wallet. He went to the carnival and spent $12. Now Sam has $5. How much was in his wallet before the carnival?

$ _?_ − $ _12_ = $ _5_

$ _12_ + $ _5_ = $ _17_

$ _17.00_

2. Morgan has $7. Her grandmother gives her a $10 bill and a $5 bill. How much money does Morgan have now?

7+10+5=22

$ _22.00_

Name _____

**Problem Solving**

## Lesson 8-5
### Reasoning

Solve & Share

Suppose you want to buy a pencil that costs 35¢. How many different ways can you use nickels, dimes, or quarters to make 35¢? Show each way. Tell how you know.

### I can ...
reason about values of coins and find different ways to make the same total value.

Mathematical Practices MP.2
Also MP.1, MP.3, MP.4, MP.8
**Content Standards** 2.MD.C.8
Also 2.OA.A.1

### Thinking Habits
What do the numbers and symbols in the problem mean?

How do the values of the coins relate to the total?

I have some quarters, dimes, and nickels. I want to buy a banana.

25¢

How many ways can I make 25¢?

**How can I reason about the different ways to make a total?**

A table can show the coins. I can use **tally marks** to record the number of coins.

**Ways to Show 25¢**

| Quarter | Dime | Nickel | Total |
|---------|------|--------|-------|
| I | | | 25¢ |
| | II | I | 25¢ |

$$25¢ = 25¢$$
$$10¢ + 10¢ + 5¢ = 25¢$$

Tally marks make it easy to show the different ways.

**Ways to Show 25¢**

| Quarter | Dime | Nickel | Total |
|---------|------|--------|-------|
| I | | | 25¢ |
| | II | I | 25¢ |
| | I | III | 25¢ |
| | | IIII I | 25¢ |

I can write an equation to show and check each way.

I can make 25¢ in 4 different ways.

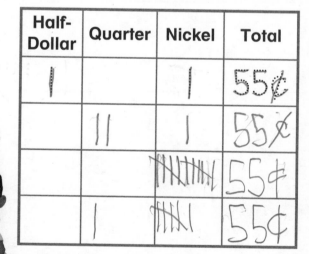

**Convince Me!** Use the chart above. Write equations to show the ways to make 25¢ using dimes and nickels.

☆ **Guided Practice** Use reasoning. Complete the table.

1. Tony wants to buy a pencil.

55¢

He has half-dollars, quarters, and nickels. Find all the ways he can make 55¢.

How do the tally marks relate to money values?

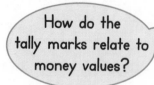

| Half-Dollar | Quarter | Nickel | Total |
|-------------|---------|--------|-------|
| I | | I | 55¢ |
| | II | I | 55¢ |
| | | IIIIIIIIIII | 55¢ |
| | I | IIIIII | 55¢ |

**Topic 8** | Lesson 5

Name _____

**Solve & Share**

What is something you do that takes about 15 minutes? What is something you can do in less than 15 minutes?

**I can …**
tell time to the nearest 5 minutes.

© **Content Standards** 2.MD.C.7 Also 2.NBT.A.2
**Mathematical Practices** MP.2, MP.5, MP.6

| 15 min. | < 15 min. |
|---|---|
| 1 center | Drinking juice |
| Calendar | Dismissal |
| Eat Little bits | Batteing at Prodigy |
| Brushing your teeth | Geting in bed |

Both clocks show 8:05.

The minute hand moves from number to number in 5 minutes.

To tell time to five minutes, start at 8:00 and count by 5s. Both clocks show 8:35.

I can start at 8:00 and count by 5s to tell the time.

There are 60 minutes in 1 hour.

The minutes start over again each hour.

**Convince Me!** The time is 9:35. Where is the hour hand?

Where is the minute hand?

**☆ Guided ☆ Practice** Complete the clocks so both clocks show the same time.

1.
 6:45

2.
 3:25

3.
 8:00

4.
  5:40

**Topic 8** | Lesson

Name _____

**Solve & Share**

Both of these clocks show the same time. How many different ways can you say this time? Write each way.

6:45

Look at the times. Count by 5s to tell the time.
What are other ways to name the same times?

Times after the half hour are often read as times before the next hour.

**1:15**  **1:30**  **1:50**  **3:30**  **3:45**  **3:50**

| 15 minutes after 1, **quarter past** 1 | 30 minutes after 1, **half past** 1 | 50 minutes after 1 | 30 minutes before 4 | 15 minutes before 4, **quarter to** 4 | 10 minutes before 4 |

**Convince Me!** Write two ways to say 5:30.

 **Guided Practice** Complete so both clocks show the same time. Then circle another way to say the time.

1.

2:30

half past 2

30 minutes before 2

2.

6:45

quarter to 7

quarter past 6

**Topic 8** | Lesson

Tools  Assessment

**ndependent Practice**

**3.**

**4:45**

_____ minutes before 5

**12:15**

quarter past _____

**2.**

**:**

25 minutes after _____

**Higher Order Thinking** Look at the clock to solve each problem.

**6.** What time will it be in 30 minutes?
Write this time in two different ways.

_____

_____

**7.** What time will it be in 50 minutes?
Write this time in two different ways.

_____

_____

8. (A-Z) **Vocabulary** Miguel is meeting a friend at **half past** 4.
Complete both clocks to show this time.

9. **Generalize** A train left the station at 6:55. What are two other ways to say this time?

_____

_____

10. **Higher Order Thinking** Draw a clock with hands that show 11:45.
Then write two ways to say the time.

_____

_____

11. ☑ **Assessment Practice** James gets home at 6:00. He starts his homework at quarter past 6. At what time does James start his homework?

Ⓐ     Ⓒ

Ⓑ     Ⓓ

**Topic 8** | Lesson

Name _____

**Solve & Share**

What is something you do in the morning? In the evening? What are some things you do in the morning and evening? Write or draw your answers.

**I can …**
tell time and use reasoning to state if the event is happening in the a.m. or p.m.

© **Content Standards** 2.MD.C.7 Also 2.NBT.A.2
**Mathematical Practices** MP.2, MP.6, MP.8

| Morning | Evening |
|---|---|
|  |  |

Morning and Evening

You can use the terms **a.m.** and **p.m.** to tell about time.

Use a.m. for morning times. I wake up at 8 a.m.

Use p.m. for afternoon or evening times. I go to bed at 8 p.m.

I eat breakfast at:

(a.m.)   p.m.

I eat lunch at school at:

(a.m.)   p.m.

I eat dinner with my family at:

a.m.   (p.m.)

**Convince Me!** What might you be doing at 6:15 a.m.? At 6:15 p.m.?

☆ **Guided Practice** ☆ Complete the clocks so both clocks show the same time. Then circle a.m. or p.m. to tell when you would do each activity.

**1.** Ride the bus to school

(a.m.)   p.m.

**2.** Do your homework

a.m.   p.m.

**Topic 8** | Lesson 8

## Independent Practice

Complete the clocks so both clocks show the same time.
Circle a.m. or p.m. to tell when you would do each activity.

**3.** Take the bus home from school

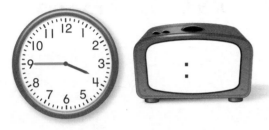

a.m.    p.m.

**4.** Walk the dog before breakfast

a.m.    p.m.

**5.** Read a book before bedtime

a.m.    p.m.

**6.** Take swimming lessons on Saturday morning

10:15

a.m.    p.m.

**7.** Watch a movie on Friday night

7:20

a.m.    p.m.

**8.** Go to a party on Saturday afternoon

2:00

a.m.    p.m.

**9. Higher Order Thinking** Jen and Maria have dance lessons at the time shown on the clock.
Write the time two different ways. Is it a.m. or p.m.? Explain.

**10.** **Be Precise** Draw hands on the clock to show what time your school begins each day. Then write the time. Include a.m. or p.m.

Time: _____

**11.** **enVision®** STEM Stargazing is looking at the stars. The best time to stargaze is on a clear moonless night.

Gina went outside to stargaze at 9:00. Is this 9:00 a.m. or 9:00 p.m.? Explain.

_____

_____

**12.** **Higher Order Thinking** Grace starts her homework at 4:15.
She finishes her homework 45 minutes later. Draw the hands on the clocks to show both times. Write both times on the digital clocks.

Circle a.m. or p.m. below to tell when Grace does her homework.

a.m.    p.m.

**13.** ☑ **Assessment Practice** Circle a.m. or p.m. to tell when you would do each activity.

Brush your teeth before bedtime     a.m.   p.m.

Walk the dog before dinner     a.m.   p.m.

Go to soccer practice after school     a.m.   p.m.

Watch the sunrise     a.m.   p.m.

**Find a Match**

Find a partner. Point to a clue. Read the clue.

Look below the clues to find a match. Write the clue letter in the box next to the match.

Find a match for every clue.

**I can ...**
add and subtract within 20.

© **Content Standard** 2.OA.B.2
**Mathematical Practices** MP.3, MP.6, MP.7, MP.8

**Clues**

**A** Is equal to 12 − 5

**B** Is equal to 9 + 2

**C** Is equal to 12 − 10

**D** Is equal to 8 + 9

**E** Is equal to 3 + 3

**F** Is equal to 15 − 7

**G** Is equal to 8 + 6

**H** Is equal to 12 − 8

**I** Is equal to 17 − 8

**J** Is equal to 6 + 9

**K** Is equal to 8 − 5

**L** Is equal to 9 + 9

| | | | | | | | |
|---|---|---|---|---|---|---|---|
| ☐ | 8 − 0 | ☐ | 10 + 8 | ☐ | 10 + 5 | ☐ | 9 + 8 |
| ☐ | 10 − 6 | ☐ | 4 + 7 | ☐ | 7 − 4 | ☐ | 3 + 4 |
| ☐ | 8 − 6 | ☐ | 9 + 5 | ☐ | 14 − 8 | ☐ | 12 − 3 |

# Vocabulary Review

Glossary

## Word List

- a.m.
- cents (¢)
- dime
- dollar
- dollar bills
- dollar sign
- greatest value
- half-dollar
- half past
- least value
- nickel
- penny
- p.m.
- quarter
- quarter past
- quarter to
- tally mark

## Understand Vocabulary

1. Circle the name of the coin with the *greatest value*.

   quarter    nickel    dime

2. Circle the name of the coin with the *least value*.

   half-dollar    penny    quarter

3. Cross out the time that is **NOT** quarter past 5 or quarter to 5.

   4:45     5:15     5:25

4. Cross out the time that is **NOT** half past 8 or quarter past 8.

   8:30     8:45     8:15

When does each event happen? Write a possible time.
Use a.m. or p.m.

5. school ends

_____

6. eat breakfast

_____

7. sunrise

_____

## Use Vocabulary in Writing

8. Explain how you can show ways to make 1 dollar (100¢) using coins. Use terms from the Word List. Give examples.

Name _____

**Set A** _____

When you count coins, start with the coin of greatest value.

Randi has the coins shown below. Count on to find the total value.

quarter (25¢)   dime (10¢)   nickel (5¢)

_25¢_   _35¢_   _40¢_

Randi has _40¢_.

**Another Example**

Duane has the coins below. How much money does Duane have?

_25¢_  _50¢_  _60¢_  _70¢_
       _70¢_

Duane has _70¢_.

Solve each problem.
Count on to find the total value.

**1.** These coins are in a jar. How many cents are in the jar?

Draw the coins in order.

Count on.   _____  _____  _____

There is _____ in the jar.

**2.** The coins shown below are in a box. How much money is in the box?

There is _____ in the box.

Dollar bills are paper money and can have different dollar values.

$1 bill
$1 = 100¢

$5 bill

$10 bill

$20 bill

$100 bill

Matt has $56. Two of his bills are $20 bills. What other bills could Matt have? You can count on to get to $56.

$20, $40, $50, $55, $56
          +$10   +$5   +$1

The other bills could be a $10 bill, a $5 bill, and a $1 bill.

---

Solve each problem.

**3.** Mr. Park has these dollar bills. Count on to find the total value.

Remember to count from the greatest bill to the least bill.

_____

**4.** A cookbook costs $36. Mrs. Beeson has a $10 bill and a $5 bill. How much more money does Mrs. Beeson need to buy the cookbook?

$_____

---

Name _____

**Set C**

**Thinking Habits**

Reasoning

What do the numbers and symbols in the problem mean?

How do the values of the coins relate to the total?

Use reasoning. Finish the table.

5. Mitch has dimes, nickels, and pennies. Find ways he can make 11¢. Show a tally mark for each coin you use.

| Dime | Nickel | Penny | Total |
|------|--------|-------|-------|
| I    |        | I     | 11¢   |
|      |        |       |       |
|      |        |       |       |
|      |        |       |       |

Did you find all the different ways?

**Set D** _____

It takes 5 minutes for the minute hand to move from one number to the next. Count on by 5s.

Read the time.
Write the same time on the digital clock.

6.

three hundred sixty-five **365**

You can say the number of minutes before the hour or after the hour.

10 minutes before 5

⟨10 minutes after 5⟩

⟨10 minutes before 5⟩

10 minutes after 5

Circle the time each clock shows.

**7.**

5 minutes before 3

5 minutes after 3

**8.**

15 minutes before 10

15 minutes after 10

Use a.m. from midnight to noon.
Use p.m. from noon to midnight.

Walking the dog before bed

Eating a morning snack

a.m.  ⟨p.m.⟩        ⟨a.m.⟩  p.m.

Circle a.m. or p.m. to tell when you would do each activity.

**9.** Afternoon recess    **10.** Feeding fish after breakfast

a.m.   p.m.        a.m.   p.m.

Name _____

**1.** Chen has these coins. How much money does Chen have? If he spends a quarter and a penny, how much money will he have? Count on to find the total.

Chen has _____ cents. He will have _____ cents.

**2.** Ellen has 4 coins that equal 46¢. She has 1 quarter, 1 dime, and 1 penny. Which is her fourth coin?

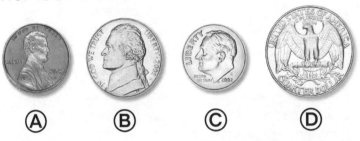

Ⓐ          Ⓑ          Ⓒ          Ⓓ

**3.** Nan has 36¢. Which coins show this?

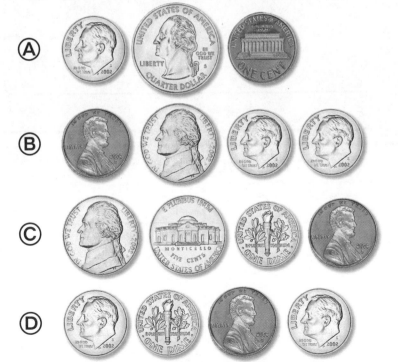

**4.** George has quarters, dimes, and nickels. Show all the ways he can make 25¢. Use tally marks.

Circle the way that uses the least number of coins.

| Ways to Show 25¢ | | | |
|---|---|---|---|
| Quarter | Dime | Nickel | Total |
|  |  |  |  |
|  |  |  |  |
|  |  |  |  |
|  |  |  |  |

5. Mr. Zink has the dollar bills shown. How many dollars does Mr. Zink have? If he spends $16 on breakfast and does not receive any change, which bills could he have used to pay for it?

6. **A.** Claire has two $20 bills, two $5 bills, and three $1 bills. Terrance has one $100 bill. How much more money does Terrance have? Explain.

**B.** What bills can you use to show how much more money Terrance has?

7. Kay has saved $30.
   Show three different ways to make $30. Use tally marks in the table at the right.

   Circle the way that uses the least number of bills.

| Ways to Show $30 | | | |
|---|---|---|---|
| $20 Bill | $10 Bill | $5 Bill | Total |
| | | | |
| | | | |
| | | | |

**8.** Sandy wakes up in the morning at the time shown on the clock.

What time does Sandy wake up?

Ⓐ 5:10 a.m

Ⓒ 5:10 p.m.

Ⓑ 6:10 a.m.

Ⓓ 6:10 p.m.

**9.** Sara's baseball game starts at the time shown on the clock.

Is this the time her game starts? Choose Yes or No.

| | | |
|---|---|---|
| 45 minutes after 4 | ◯ Yes | ◯ No |
| 15 minutes before 5 | ◯ Yes | ◯ No |
| quarter to 4 | ◯ Yes | ◯ No |
| quarter to 5 | ◯ Yes | ◯ No |

**10.** The clock shows the time that Holly arrives to school. What time does the clock show? Choose all that apply.

☐ half past 7

☐ quarter past 8

☐ 30 minutes after 8

☐ half past 8

☐ 15 minutes to 9

**11.** The first clock shows the time the sun rises. Write the same time on the second clock. Then circle a.m. or p.m.

a.m.   p.m.

**12.** Look at the time on the first clock. Write that time on the second clock.

**13.** Circle a.m. or p.m. to tell when you would do each activity.

Watch the sunset at 7:40.　　　　a.m.　p.m.

Take a music lesson after school.　a.m.　p.m.

Brush your teeth before school.　　a.m.　p.m.

Eat breakfast at 6:45.　　　　　a.m.　p.m.

**14.** Draw lines to match the time on each clock in the first row to the same time shown in the second row.

**Topic 8** | Assessment Practice

Name _____

## The Toy Store
Terry's family owns a toy store.
These are some of the things
they sell.

$14
$21
$1
38¢

**1.** Lorna buys the crayons with 6 coins.
Ken buys the crayons with 7 coins.
Draw the coins that each of them used.

| Lorna's 6 coins | Ken's 7 coins |
|---|---|
| | |

**2.** Kim goes to the toy store
with these coins.

**Part A** What is the total value of the coins
Kim has? Explain how you know.

_____

_____

_____

**Part B** How much more money does Kim
need to buy the book? Explain.

**3.** Kay's father buys a toy train at the toy store for $50.

**Part A**

Show five different ways that he could have paid $50. Use tally marks to complete the table.

| Ways to Show $50 | | | |
|---|---|---|---|
| $20 Bill | $10 Bill | $5 Bill | Total |
| | | | $50 |
| | | | $50 |
| | | | $50 |
| | | | $50 |
| | | | $50 |

**Part B**

Which way uses the least number of bills to make $50? Explain.

**4.** Ted walks to the toy store in the afternoon.

**Part A**

He starts walking at the time shown on the digital clock. Draw hands on the second clock to show the same time.

Is the time on the clocks above 3:35 a.m. or 3:35 p.m.? Explain how you know.

**Part B**

Write the time on the clocks in two different ways.

# Glossary

## A

### add

When you add, you join groups together.

$$3 + 4 = 7$$

### addend

numbers that are added

$$2 + 5 = 7$$

↑ ↑

addends

### after

424 comes after 423.

| 420 | 421 | 422 | 423 | 424 | 425 | 426 | 427 | 428 | 429 |
|-----|-----|-----|-----|-----|-----|-----|-----|-----|-----|

### a.m.

clock time from midnight until noon

### angle

the corner shape formed by two sides that meet

### array

a group of objects set in equal rows and columns that forms a rectangle

## B

### bar diagram

a model for addition and subtraction that shows the parts and the whole

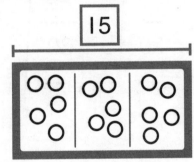

### bar graph

A bar graph uses bars to show data.

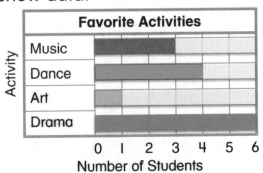

Glossary

**G1**

## before

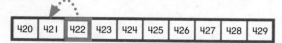

421 comes before 422.

## break apart

You can break apart a number into its place value parts.

$$27 + 35 = ?$$

Tens: 20    30

Ones: 7    5

## centimeter (cm)

a metric unit of length that is part of 1 meter

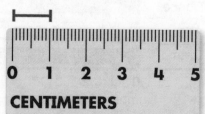

**CENTIMETERS**

## cents

The value of a coin is measured in cents (¢).

1 cent (¢)   10 cents (¢)

## coins

money that is made out of metal and that can have different values

1¢    5¢    10¢    25¢    50¢

## column

objects in an array or data in a table that are shown up and down

column

| 1 | 2 | 3 | 4 | 5 |
|---|---|---|---|---|
| 11 | 12 | 13 | 14 | 15 |
| 21 | 22 | 23 | 24 | 25 |
| 31 | 32 | 33 | 34 | 35 |

## compare

When you compare numbers, you find out if a number is greater than, less than, or equal to another number.

147 ⃝> 143

147 is greater than 143.

## compatible numbers

numbers that are easy to add or subtract using mental math

$$8 + 2$$
$$20 + 7$$
$$53 - 10$$

## compensation

a mental math strategy you can use to add or subtract

$$38 + 24 = ?$$
$$+ 2 \quad - 2$$

You add 2 to 38 to make 40. Then subtract 2 from 24 to get 22. 40 + 22 = 62. So, 38 + 24 = 62.

## cube

a solid figure with six faces that are matching squares

## data

information you collect and can be shown in a table or graph

| Favorite Fruit | |
|---|---|
| Apple | 7 |
| Peach | 4 |
| Orange | 5 |

## decrease

to become lesser in value

$$600 \longrightarrow 550$$

600 decreased by 50 is 550.

## difference

the answer in a subtraction equation or problem

$$14 - 6 = 8$$

↑

difference

## digits

Numbers are made up of 1 or more digits. 43 has 2 digits.

## dime

10 cents or 10¢

## dollar

One dollar equals 100¢.

## dollar bills

paper money that can have different dollar values, such as $1, $5, $10, $20, or $100

## dollar sign

a symbol used to show that a number represents money

$37

↑

dollar sign

## doubles

addition facts that have two addends that are the same

$$4 + 4 = 8$$

addend   addend

## edge

a line formed where two faces of a solid figure meet

edge

## equal shares

parts of a whole that are the same size

All 4 shares are equal.

## equals (=)

has the same value

$$36 = 36$$

36 is equal to 36.

## equation

a math sentence that uses an equal sign (=) to show that the value on the left is equal to the value on the right

$$3 + ? = 7$$

$$14 - 6 = 8$$

## estimate

When you estimate, you make a good guess.

38 + 41 is about 80.

This table is about 3 feet long.

## even

a number that can be shown as two equal groups of cubes.

8 is even.

## expanded form

a way of writing a number that shows the place value of each digit

$$400 + 60 + 3 = 463$$

## face

a flat surface of a solid figure that does not roll

face

## fact family

a group of related addition and subtraction facts

$$2 + 4 = 6$$
$$4 + 2 = 6$$
$$6 - 2 = 4$$
$$6 - 4 = 2$$

## foot (ft)

a standard unit of length equal to 12 inches

## fourths

When a whole is divided into 4 equal shares, the shares are called fourths.

## fraction

a number, such as $\frac{1}{2}$ or $\frac{3}{4}$, that names part of a whole or part of a set

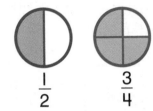

$\frac{1}{2}$      $\frac{3}{4}$

G

## greater than (>)

has greater value

$$5 > 1$$

5 is greater than 1.

## greatest

the number in a group of numbers that has the largest value

35  47  58  (61)
greatest

## greatest value

The coin that has the greatest value is the coin that is worth the most.

The quarter has the greatest value.

H

## half-dollar

50 cents or 50¢

## half past

30 minutes past the hour

It is half past 9.

## halves (half)

When a whole is divided into 2 equal shares, the shares are called halves.

## height

how tall an object is from bottom to top

## hexagon

a polygon that has 6 sides

## hour

An hour is 60 minutes.

## hundred

10 tens make 1 hundred.

## I

## inch (in.)

a standard unit of length that is part of 1 foot

## increase

to become greater in value

550 ⟶ 600

550 increased by 50 is 600.

## L

## least

the number in a group of numbers that has the smallest value

35 47 58 61
↳ least

## least value

The coin that has the least value is the coin that is worth the least.

The dime has the least value.

## length

the distance from one end to the other end of an object

## less than (<)

has less value

2 < 6

2 is less than 6.

## line plot

A line plot uses dots or Xs above a number line to show data.

**Lengths of Shells**

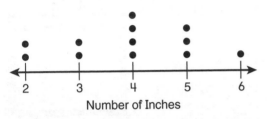

Number of Inches

Start at 23. Count on 2 tens. 33, 43

### mental math

math you do in your head

$$23 + 20 = 43$$

### meter (m)

a metric unit of length equal to 100 centimeters

A long step is about a meter.

## minute

a standard length of time

There are 60 minutes in 1 hour.

### near doubles

addition facts that have two addends that are close

$$4 + 5 = 9$$

addend   addend

## nearest centimeter

The whole number centimeter mark closest to the measure is the nearest centimeter.

about 2 cm long

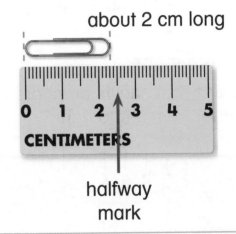

CENTIMETERS

halfway mark

### nearest inch

The whole number inch mark closest to the measure is the nearest inch.

about 2 inches long

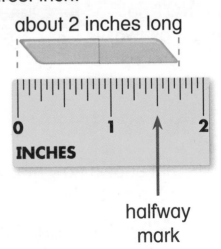

INCHES

halfway mark

## nickel

5 cents or 5¢

## number line

a line that shows numbers in order from left to right

## O

## odd

a number that can **NOT** be shown as two equal groups of cubes

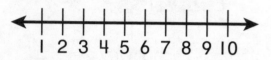

9 is odd.

## ones

digits that shows how many ones are in a number

$$54 + 14 = 68$$

↑    ↑    ↑

## open number line

An open number line is a tool that can help you add or subtract. It can begin at any number.

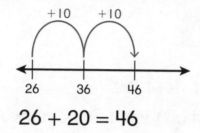

$$26 + 20 = 46$$

## order

to place numbers from least to greatest or from greatest to least

least    greatest

## P

## part

a piece of a whole or of a number

2 and 3 are parts of 5.

## partial difference

When you subtract numbers, you can subtract amounts that total the number you are subtracting. The differences you find as you complete each subtraction are called partial differences.

```
   72
 − 20
 ────
   52
 −  2
 ────
   50
 −  2
 ────
   48
```

For example, when finding 72 − 24, 52 and 50 are partial differences.

## partial sum

When you add numbers, the sum of one of the place values is a partial sum.

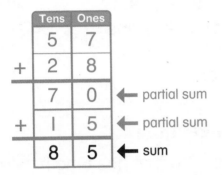

| Tens | Ones | |
|------|------|---|
| 5 | 7 | |
| + 2 | 8 | |
| 7 | 0 | ← partial sum |
| + 1 | 5 | ← partial sum |
| 8 | 5 | ← sum |

## penny

1 cent or 1¢

## pentagon

a polygon that has 5 sides

## picture graph

a graph that uses pictures to show data

| Favorite Ball Games | |
|---------|------------|
| Baseball |  |
| Soccer | |
| Tennis | |

Each = 1 student

## place-value chart

a chart matches each digit of a number with its place

| Hundreds | Tens | Ones |
|----------|------|------|
| 3 | 4 | 8 |

## plane shape

a flat shape

circle   rectangle   square   triangle

## p.m.

clock time from noon until midnight

7:10 PM

## polygon

a closed plane shape with 3 or more sides

 Q

## quadrilateral

a polygon that has 4 sides

## quarter

25 cents or 25¢

## quarter past

15 minutes after the hour

4:15

It is quarter past 4.

## quarter to

15 minutes before the hour

It is quarter to 4.

## regroup

to name a number or part in a different way

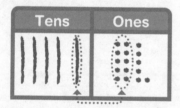

10 ones can be regrouped as 1 ten. 1 ten can be regrouped as 10 ones.

## related

Addition facts and subtraction facts are related if they have the same numbers.

$$2 + 3 = 5$$
$$5 - 2 = 3$$

## right angle

an angle that forms a square corner

## row

objects in an array or data in a table that are shown across

| 1 | 2 | 3 | 4 | 5 |
|---|---|---|---|---|
| 11 | 12 | 13 | 14 | 15 | ← row
| 21 | 22 | 23 | 24 | 25 |
| 31 | 32 | 33 | 34 | 35 |

## side

a line segment that makes one part of a plane shape

side

## solid figure

a shape that has length, width, and height

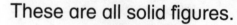  

These are all solid figures.

## standard form

a way to write a number using only digits

436

## subtract

When you subtract, you find out how many are left or which group has more.

$$5 - 3 = 2$$

## sum

the answer to an addition equation or problem

$$3 + 4 = \boxed{7}$$

$$\begin{array}{r} 4 \\ + 3 \\ \hline 7 \end{array}$$

sum $\longrightarrow$ 7

## symbol

a picture or character that stands for something

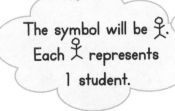

The symbol will be ⚲.
Each ⚲ represents 1 student.

---

 **T**

## tally mark

a symbol used to keep track of each piece of information in an organized list

| Ways to Show 30¢ | | | |
|---|---|---|---|
| Quarter | Dime | Nickel | Total |
| I | | I | 30¢ |
| | III | | 30¢ |
| | II | II | 30¢ |
| | I | IIII | 30¢ |
| | | IIII I | 30¢ |

## tens

the digit that shows how many groups of ten are in a number

2**3**8

## thirds

When a whole is divided into 3 equal shares, the shares are called thirds.

---

## thousand

10 hundreds make 1 thousand.

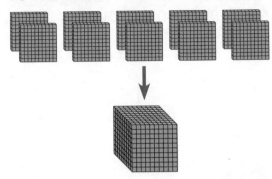

 **U**

## unequal

Unequal parts are parts that are not equal.

5 unequal parts

## unit

You can use different units to measure.

about 12 inches
about 1 foot

**unknown**

a symbol that stands for a number in an equation

$$34 + ? = 67$$

↑

unknown

**vertices (vertex)**

corner points where 2 sides of a polygon meet or where edges of a solid figure meet

vertex

**whole**

a single unit that can be divided into parts

The two halves make one whole circle.

**width**

the distance across an object

**word form**

a way to write a number using only words

The word form for 23 is twenty-three.

**yard (yd)**

a standard unit of length equal to 3 feet

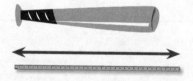

A baseball bat is about a yard long.

# Photographs

Every effort has been made to secure permission and provide appropriate credit for photographic material. The publisher deeply regrets any omission and pledges to correct errors called to its attention in subsequent editions.

Unless otherwise acknowledged, all photographs are the property of Savvas Learning Company LLC.

Photo locators denoted as follows: Top (T), Center (C), Bottom (B), Left (L), Right (R), Background (Bkgd)

**1** (TL) Africa Studio/Fotolia, (TC) Africa Studio/Fotolia, (TR) karandaev/Fotolia, (BL) Lori Martin/Shutterstock; (BR) An Nguyen/Shutterstock, **3** (T) 123RF, (C) Sean Pavone/Shutterstock, (B) Trinet Uzun/Shutterstock; **4** (Bkgrd) Russo Photography/Shutterstock, (T) Sergey Sarychev/Shutterstock, (C) Lesinka372/Shutterstock, (B) Corinna Huter/Shutterstock, 123RF; **57** (TL) Shadowmac/Shutterstock, (TR) Rose Thompson/Shutterstock, (BL) Tory Kallman/Shutterstock, (BR) Jo Crebbin/Shutterstock; **59** (T) Steve Byland/Shutterstock, (B) Islavicek/Shutterstock; **60** (T) Smileus/Shutterstock, (B) 123RF; **89** (L) FiCo74/Fotolia; (R) Antonio Scarpi/Fotolia, **91** (T) Pisaphotography/Shutterstock, (C) Aviation Images/Alamy Stock Photo, (B) Lazyllama/Shutterstock; **92** (Bkgrd) 123RF, S_Rouse/Shutterstock; **133** Beboy/Shutterstock; **135** (T) Echo/Juice Images/Getty Images, (B) Peter Leahy/Shutterstock; **136** (T) Universal Images Group North America LLC/Alamy Stock Photo, (B) Charles O. Cecil/Alamy Stock Photo; **185** Deborah Benbrook/Fotolia; **187** (T) Cturtletrax/iStock/Getty Images, (C) Inxti/Shutterstock, (B) Horizon International Images Limited/Alamy Stock Photo; **188** (Bkgrd) Evgeny Atamanenko/Shutterstock, (T) Nisakorn Neera/Shutterstock, (B) Thomas M Perkins/Shutterstock; **233** GlebStock/Shutterstock; **235** (T) Joe McDonald/Corbis Documentary/Getty Images, (B) Hero Images Inc./Alamy Stock Photo; **236** (T) Charles Wollertz/123RF, (B) Vchal/Shutterstock; **277** Paylessimages/Fotolia; **279** (T) Kiselev Andrey Valerevich/Shutterstock, (C) Mr. Ned Klezmer/Shutterstock, (B) IrinaK/Shutterstock; **280** (Bkgrd) Mikhail Zahranichny/Shutterstock, Good Shop Background/Shutterstock; **325** Ambient Ideas/Shutterstock; **327** (T) Chuck Pefley/Alamy Stock Photo, (B) Masterchief_Productions; **328** (B) (T) Will Hart/PhotoEdit, Christopher Villano/Image Source/Alamy Stock Photo; **331** B Brown/Shutterstock; **363** B Brown/Shutterstock; **367** B Brown/Shutterstock; **373** Es0lex/Fotolia; **375** (T) Christos Georghiou/Shutterstock, (C) Gilles Barbier/imageBROKER/Alamy Stock Photo, (B) Brian J. Skerry/National Geographic/Getty Images; **376** (Bkgrd) People Image Studio/Shutterstock, (T) Fashion iconography/Shutterstock; (B) Brandon Alms/Shutterstock; **429** Tonyz20/Shutterstock; **431** (T) Karin Hildebrand Lau/Alamy Stock Photo, (B) Richard Paul Kane/Shutterstock; **432** (T) CharlieTong/Getty Images, (B) Corey Rich/Aurora Photos/Alamy Stock Photo; **469** Klagyivik Viktor/Shutterstock; **471** (T) Felix Lipov/Shutterstock, (C) Skynesher/Vetta/Getty Images, (B) Stephen Vincent/Alamy Stock Photo; **472** (Bkgrd) Sergiy Bykhunenko/Shutterstock, Gino Santa Maria/Shutterstock; **505** Ant Clausen/Fotolia; **507** (T) Peter Bernik/Shutterstock, (B) Westlee Jay Appleton/Shutterstock; **508** (T) Samuel Borges Photography/Shutterstock, (B) Steven Hogg/Shutterstock; **557** Yurakr/Shutterstock; **559** (T) EFesenko/Shutterstock, (C) Franck Boston/Shutterstock, (B) Creeed/Shutterstock; **560** (Bkgrd) SuriyaPhoto/Shutterstock, Studio Kiwi/Shutterstock, **568** StudioSmart/Shutterstock; **605** Bonita R. Cheshier/Shutterstock; **607** (T) Angelo Ferraris/Shutterstock, (B) Tanawat Palee/Shutterstock; **608** (B) Naramit/Shutterstock; (T) Business stock/Shutterstock, **628** Lledó/Fotolia; **637** (R) Ivonne Wierink/Fotolia, (L) Karichs/Fotolia; **639** (T) Karamysh/Shutterstock, (C) Noxnorthys/Shutterstock, (B) Gabriele Maltinti/Shutterstock; **640** (Bkgrd) Bowie15/123RF, Koya979/Shutterstock